Teaching Riding

Diane S. Solomon

Drawings by William R. Culbertson

and Ann Williams

Photographs by Robert G. Harvey,

and Kris Illenberger

Teaching Riding

Step-by-Step Schooling
for Horse and Rider

University of Oklahoma Press : Norman

Library of Congress Cataloging in
Publication Data

Solomon, Diane S. (Diane Schilling), 1943–
    Teaching riding.

    Bibliography: p. 159.
    Includes index.
    1. Horsemanship—Study and teaching.
2. Horsemanship.   3. Dressage.   I. Title.
SF310.5.S64   798.2'3   81–40281
                                   AACR2

*Blessed are the few who find a friend
who allows them the freedom to live
and be without imposing change; who
appreciates and respects the awesome
beauty of nature and loves from the
depths of his heart the music of the wind,
rain, and thunder and knows, too, the
smile and the warmth of the sun.*

This book is dedicated to such a friend . . .
CHARLES EAGLE PLUME

Contents

Illustrations

APPENDICES

Preface

This book is designed to provide methodical sequential techniques for those engaged in teaching horsemanship. Although the book has been developed for use in instruction in English riding, most of the material presented in the beginning and intermediate parts is also applicable to the training of the western horse and rider. While this book was written primarily for university application, it can easily be adapted to any instructional-program format.

My Gratitude . . .

To the Animal Sciences Department of Colorado State University, and particularly to past and present administrators, Terry R. Greathouse, Bernard M. Jones, and Carey L. Quarles, for making this book possible.

To Kay Meredith, Elliot Abhau, and the staff at Meredith Manor, who taught me the meaning of work and perseverance and the science and art of equitation.

To Bill Culbertson, for his continual help in many equestrian endeavors.

To Gary Greathouse, for his support in equitation activities.

To my students, who provided me with a testing ground for this material.

To those who helped me finish this book, Joy Colbert and Helen Wigdahl, for secretarial and editorial assistance.

Forward-seat photographs are of Dani SerVoss on King Chanticleer, Fort Collins, Colorado. Balanced-seat photographs are of the author on Rolyn Red.

DIANE S. SOLOMON
Fort Collins, Colorado

Teaching Riding

Introduction

The following comments and suggestions are offered to aid the instructor in organizing the equitation program.

Class Organization

One instructor can effectively work with eight or nine riders in a class. If the instructor works with an assistant, ten to twelve riders can be given adequate attention. Ideally a class consists of fourteen to fifteen riders with an instructor and two or three assistant instructors. It is important to have enough instructors to allow the students to work in small groups and receive individual attention.

At the first class period students should be asked to complete a 3-by-5 index card with the following information: name, address, telephone number, riding background, career goal (horse-oriented?), riding interests, and approximate height and weight. This information is used in making the first horse assignments. Although assignments should be changed if an obvious rider-horse conflict arises, it is best to allow a student to ride a horse four or five times to become familiar with his particular problems and way of going before deciding to change horses.

For each class of fifteen horses two or three rotation horses will be needed. The horses should be taught to lunge easily and quietly so that the students, beginners through advanced, can work to develop the seat and aids without the added concern of controlling the horse.

Approximately two hours will be needed for a class period, if the students are expected to catch the horse, tack up, ride, and then cool out, comfort-groom, and put the horse away. It is suggested that the students perform these duties themselves. It is not uncommon to find a student who has no idea how to prepare a horse for a riding lesson and take care of him afterward.

The time to be allowed for each activity is approximately as follows:

Short lecture: 15 to 20 minutes
Catch and tack up: 15 to 20 minutes for beginners, 10 minutes for intermediate and advanced riders
Lesson: 45 minutes to 1 hour
Cool out: 10 minutes
Untack and put away: 15 minutes

Each class should begin with a mini-lecture. During this time the instructor introduces new material or reviews previous material and answers questions. Students must first understand the theory and aids before trying to convey their wishes to the horse. Presenting new material *before* students are mounted allows them to concentrate on the theory. Diagrams should be placed on a chalkboard, and a demonstration should follow to provide a visual concept of what the students will strive to achieve.

Arena Requirements

A large arena with rectangular dimensions and good footing should be provided as a main work area. It is helpful if the arena can be divided into two smaller arenas by placing cavalletti across the middle, bisecting the arena into two equal parts. Using this setup, an instructor can work between two groups of students and supervise assistant instructors without leaving one arena to go to another. A dressage arena with the appropriate letters should also be available.

Footing in both arenas should be moderate, approximately 3 to 4 inches of loose footing—half sand and half shavings—mixed with light oil. Hard footing increases concussion to the horse's legs, and heavy (sandy) or deep footing will tend to overwork the joints and tendons in the legs, making it difficult for the horse to perform lateral movements or jump without incurring undue physical stress.

Horses

Many pure breeds and/or mixtures of breeds make good school horses. If possible, examples of the different breeds should be available to acquaint students with distinctive breed characteristics. Horses of adequate size (15 hands), with good disposition, ample bone, and good feet are of utmost importance. Generally speaking, horses that tend to be high-strung and "flighty" do not serve well. Since school horses are handled by a number of different students every day, some horses tend to become resentful when groundwork and riding are not performed in a consistent manner. For this reason a horse's disposition should be carefully evaluated before purchase.

When possible it is best to have one group of horses for work in the beginning and intermediate riding classes and another for work in the intermediate and advanced classes or only the advanced classes. With this arrangement students progress to the more highly trained horses and retain their enthusiasm for riding. At the same time, the attitude of the advanced horses remains stable, and they continue to work well as skilled students ride them.

PURCHASING SCHOOL HORSES

School horses are expensive to purchase; therefore, it is best to acquire horses that are six to eight years old to help ensure as long a work life as possible. Young horses, three to five years old, that have been started under saddle and are quiet but are *not* certain of their basic work should not be used in an equitation program. Such horses tend to become confused quickly when improper aids are given. If a horse is considered a "good find," then the instructor should ride the horse until there is no question regarding his basic knowledge and way of going. This procedure will develop a willing attitude in the horse and eventually allow him to become a valuable school horse.

At the time of purchase each horse should tie and stand quietly, walk, trot, canter, and halt without undue restraint. Once a school or riding program has become established, horses may be donated. In this instance an older horse, say twelve years old, may provide an excellent beginner mount for his remaining work years. Such horses can make a valuable contribution to a riding program.

If horses are housed in sheltered pens accommodating approximately six to seven head, a new horse should be able to adapt quietly to this arrangement. Some horses thrive when stalled individually but lose their thrifty condition in a herd.

TACK, SERVICES, AND FEES

If all equipment is provided for the students, the cost of upkeep, repair, and replacement of equipment, as well as feed, farrier service, and routine veterinary care must be considered when establishing the class fee. Maintenance must always be taken into account; and failure to do so will rapidly deplete the operating fund.

CHECKLIST

A good equitation program is built on good instruction and a sound working knowledge of horse-management practices. If either is missing, the program will be much less than first-rate. Make a checklist and be sure to include all the items listed below to help ensure success:

1. Purchase sound horses with good dispositions.
2. Feed quality rations and provide good health care.
3. Provide routine farrier service.
4. Provide adequate housing with a constant source of water.
5. Provide an adequate working arena with proper footing for all levels of riding.
6. Employ instructors who are patient and kind but decisive enough to control a group and instill confidence and desire in riders.
7. Develop well-organized lesson plans.
8. Provide enough instructors to handle groups effectively.

Note on Photographs

The photographs in this book are not intended to illustrate perfection. Each picture represents an instant in the horse's workout—an instant that is preceded or followed by a good to less desirable moment for the horse and rider. Each photograph is intended to represent an acceptable working frame for the horse and an adequate position for the rider.

May we all continue to reach toward perfection as we ride and work horses. May next year find us more skillful in "feeling" an art that is difficult to express in words.

Definitions

Throughout this book the term "inside" refers to the direction of the horse's bend. The term "outside" refers to the outside of the horse's bend. If a horse is bent to the left, the left aids are the inside aids, and the right aids are the outside aids. The terms have nothing to do with the position of the horse as it relates to the arena wall.

Part One

Elementary
Equitation

Chapter 1

Basic Handling

The first part of this book is designed to help teachers acquaint students with proper horse-handling procedures, the basics of correct equitation, and the footfall patterns and aids for the horse's three natural gaits. Firm understanding and application of this knowledge are necessary for advancement to the finer points of riding.

Safety Measures

Recommended safety dress requirements for all students are a hard hat, long pants, shirt, and shoes with hard soles and heels. Hiking boots or boots with waffle soles are not permitted because they will not slide easily out of stirrups in an emergency. Preferred attire includes a hard hat, breeches, a suitable shirt or turtleneck, English boots, and gloves.

For the student's safety and to comply with the insurance regulations commonly imposed, a minimal dress code must be enforced (see Appendix F). When outlining the necessity of working safely around horses, it is important to establish a set of safety rules and distribute a rules list among the students. In a university or other structured setting a safety-rules test should be administered every three or four months to maintain a high level of safety awareness among students. It will also help protect the instructional program from unnecessary litigation. See Appendix D for a sample safety-rules handout and Appendix E for a sample safety-rules test.

Approaching the Horse

Emphasize that the student must always let the horse know that someone is approaching by speaking to get his attention. A surprise approach can result in a frightened horse planting a defensive kick and causing serious injury to the student.

Fig. 1. Whenever possible, approach a horse at a three-quarter angle to his shoulder.

Horses that are not tied in a box stall should be approached at a three-quarter angle to the animal's shoulder (fig. 1). At this position the horse can best see a person coming toward him. Approaching a horse directly from the front or rear is never advisable. A horse is unable to see clearly what is directly in front of him or directly behind his hindquarters because of his limited visual field owing to the location and functioning apparatus of his eyes. Whenever possible, the horse is approached from the left side since this is the traditional side from which horses are handled.

It is of utmost importance that a horse housed in a tie stall be made aware of an approaching person. Students should be taught to speak to the horse first and then place the right hand on the horse's left hip and adjust the animal's position to the right. Then they enter on the left side and quietly approach the horse's head.

Use of the tie stall is not recommended because of the reduced safety factor for students working in such a confined area. They may, however, provide the only economical solution to keeping many horses at a stalled school.

Haltering

When approaching a horse, the student carries the halter and attached rope neatly in the left hand. The halter is unbuckled and ready to be put on. On reaching the left side of the horse, the student puts the halter rope around the horse's neck and places the right arm across the top of the neck, grasping the crownpiece and bringing it up behind the ears so that it extends down the left side of the head. The student uses the right hand to hold the crownpiece in place while with the left hand raising the halter over the nose. Last, the nosepiece is adjusted on the bridge of the nose, and the halter is buckled on the left side of the head.

When properly adjusted, all parts of the halter should fit close to the horse's head, with only a small space allowing the insertion of two fingers between the horse's throat and the halter. If the halter hangs too far down the nose and is loose in the throat area, the horse may rub off the halter over his head. Too tight an adjustment results in discomfort and undue restraint.

Placing the halter over the horse's neck *first* and over the nose second is the preferred method of haltering because it establishes a measure of control over the horse's movement. Should the horse try to walk away, the student is able to restrain him. If the halter is dropped first over the nose, the horse is able to free himself by quickly backing a few steps, turning, and moving away. Control is the key, and proper haltering is a good way to establish it.

Leading

The student should always walk close to the horse's left shoulder (fig. 2). This is the safest position and the one from which the handler can exert maximum control. The right hand should be placed on the rope approximately eight to twelve inches from the halter. The rest of the rope should be folded in a figure eight or coiled loosely and carried in the left hand. The lead rope should never be coiled snugly around the hand; a startled horse could jump backward and pull the rope tight around it.

A student leading a horse with a slack rope and walking in front of the horse or toward the rear is in a dangerous position. In either position the horse is the one in control and can pull the student with him.

Grooming

During grooming, the student should be concerned with removing dirt and dust accumulations while also checking for minor cuts, bruises, and other abnormal conditions. A daily visual check of a

Fig. 2. Walking close to the horse's left shoulder is the safest position for leading and allows the handler to exert the most control over the horse.

horse's condition and soundness is one of the best ways to catch little problems and keep them from becoming big ones.

Complete grooming aids include a rubber curry comb, soft- and medium-textured brushes, a hoof-pick, a small wire brush, a sponge, two towels, water, hoof dressing, and baby oil. When thorough grooming is desired, the procedure outlined below should be followed:

1. The rubber curry comb or grooming mitt is used in a firm, circular motion to loosen surface dust and dirt from the horse's coat. Do not use the curry comb on the face or below the knees and hocks; there is little flesh on those portions of the body to cushion the raking effect of the curry comb. Beginning at the back of the ears, the groom should work toward the hindquarters, paying particular attention to the back and heart girth, the areas covered by equipment during work under saddle. Removal of dirt is vital; if it is ignored, particles of debris can be ground into the skin, causing saddle sores and girth galls. A special comb or a brush with stiff bristles is used on the mane and tail to remove tangles.

2. A brush of medium texture is used to remove loosened dirt from the hair coat. Beginning in the back of the ears and working toward the hindquarters, use this brush with short, vigorous strokes in the direction of the lay of the hair. To help ensure removal of dirt, the groom should flick the wrist with an outward twist so that the dirt is propelled from the hair and not just relocated by long nonenergetic brushstrokes. This brush should not be used on the face or below the knees or hocks. Use a softer brush to guard against discomfort and ensure the horse's continued pleasure in the grooming process.

3. A soft brush is used around the horse's head, eyes, and ears. It may also be used on the lower portions of the legs and in the pastern area. Use a damp sponge followed with a soft cloth to cleanse and dry the eyes and nostrils. After brushing, rub the horse down from head to tail with a soft towel to remove the final particles of dirt and dust from the coat.

4. A hoof-pick is used to clean the horse's feet before and after the work period. Removal of debris is essential to keep the feet in a healthy condition. If debris is allowed to remain packed in the feet, especially around the sides of the frog, an anaerobic bacterial condition known as thrush may develop. The black, offensive-smelling oozing discharge can cause lameness and degeneration of the frog in untreated cases. Nonhygienic surroundings, poorly managed stalls, and lack of correct frog pressure caused by improper shoeing or trimming also contribute to the occurrence of this disease.

To prevent thrush, the feet should be cleaned with a hoof-pick at least once a day. Then use a small wire brush and water to scrub the frog and sole. A commercial hoof dressing can be applied before the horse is returned to his stall or pen. Although this topical application does not add moisture to the feet, it helps the feet retain their own moisture. During extremely dry periods it may be necessary to apply hoof dressing daily. Brush hoof dressing on all areas of the foot, giving special care to the coronary band, where growth originates, and to the bulbs of the heel, frog, and sole, which must remain pliable to provide the foot structure with an adequate supply of blood to keep it functioning properly.

5. A light application of baby oil may be rubbed into the base of the mane, tail, and forelock to help prevent dryness and to encourage the hairs to lie flat. Applying baby oil to the hocks and elbows also helps prevent dry skin and unsightly scaling.

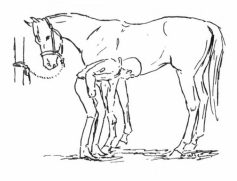

BILL CULBERTSON

Fig. 3. Pick up a horse's feet safely and with control.

Picking Up the Horse's Feet

The horse's feet should be picked up methodically, authoritatively, safely, and with control (fig. 3). To pick up a front foot, the student stands at the horse's shoulder facing the rear quarters. The hand closest to the horse should be run down the back of the leg and around the front of the fetlock joint. If the student leans into the horse's shoulder, the horse will shift his weight to the other side. This should provide ample pressure for a well-trained horse to pick up his foot. If the horse does not respond, the tendon running down the back of the leg may be pinched just above the fetlock joint. As the horse lifts his foot, the student should secure it against the inside portion of his knee, or, if preferred, the student may step across the raised leg and hold the horse's pastern area securely between his knees, his own feet being arranged in a pigeon-toed position. The foot is now in a safe position to clean, shoe, or medicate. The foot should be held by the toe for maximum control. Should the horse try to pull away, the toe may be flexed toward the fetlock joint to restrain his movement. Use the hoof-pick to remove debris from the sole and frog area. Hold it so that the pointed portion of the pick is toward the toe. The pick is used from heel to toe to prevent injury or puncturing the bulbs of the heel. When the foot has been cleaned, it should be released slowly, allowing the horse to replace it on the ground. Never drop the foot suddenly; to do so would contribute to a horse's nervousness and distrust since he would never know when his foot would be released.

To pick up a hind foot, place the hand on the horse's hip, push against it, and slide the other hand down the back of the leg, over the hock, and to the middle of the cannon bone. Now pull the leg straight forward and lift it off the ground. Step under and then ahead and slightly to the rear of the horse, resting the fetlock between the knees. Place the near arm around the inside of the leg so that the elbow and the horse's hock are in approximately the same location. The hind foot is also held by the toe. This "hammerlock" position provides the largest margin of safety when a student is working with a young or uncooperative horse. Keeping the hand against the horse's hip is a safety factor that helps brace the student when picking up a leg and also makes it easier to push the body away if a horse tries to kick.

Saddling

The student should be encouraged to use a clean, soft, washable, fleece-type pad under the saddle. Before placing it on the horse's back, examine the pad for foreign material that could cause back injuries. Stand on the left side of the horse and place the pad on the horse's neck just in front of the withers; then move it backward into place to ensure that the hair remains smooth under the pad and saddle. Once the pad is in place, the saddle should be lifted and gently placed — not disrespectfully dropped — on the horse's back. Grasp the pommel with the right hand, slightly elevating the saddle so that the front portion of the pad is lifted up into the gullet of the saddle, allowing the withers maximum freedom of movement. A tight saddle pad over the withers affects a horse the way

a tight shirt over the shoulders affects a human being. The result is the same: restricted movement and impaired performance and, for horses, the possibility of injury to the withers with prolonged use.

When various saddles are used interchangeably by many students, care must be taken to ensure that the saddle fits each horse and does not sit down too close to the horse's withers. Should an ill-fitting saddle go unnoticed, a horse can suffer from uncomfortable pressure and even fistulated withers, a condition characterized by painful open sores. If the saddle sits too low on the withers, the condition can be rectified by the addition of an extra pad until the saddle can be changed.

A bounce pad, a round pad made of foam rubber, should be placed under the back of the saddle to raise it to a level position and add protective cushioning to the horse's back (see Appendix G).

After the saddle has been placed on the horse's back and adjusted, the girth is then attached to the billet straps on the right side of the saddle and then secured on the left side just tightly enough to hold the saddle in place. Pulling the girth tight in one quick action causes a horse to become "cinchy," a common name given to a horse that rings his tail, flattens his ears, opens his mouth, and expresses general dissatisfaction. No human being would voluntarily jerk a belt uncomfortably tight around the middle; the same consideration should be extended to the horse. When the girth is fully secured, the middle seam should be very close to the center of the heart girth. Approximately half the girth should be on one side of the horse, and half on the other side to maintain equal pressure, balance, and comfort.

Bridling

As with all other basic handling procedures, the horse should be bridled from the left side. If the animal is haltered and tied, free the rope, unbuckle the halter, and place the rope over the neck. This keeps the halter out of the way during the bridling process and also allows for some measure of control should the horse move before the bridle is in place.

Release the bridle from its stored figure-eight position and lift it along the side of the head so that the crownpiece is at the proper height behind the ears. If the bit fails to extend downward far enough to the horse's mouth, lengthen the bridle before attempting to bridle the horse. A bridle that is a little longer than necessary can be more comfortably corrected once in place than one that is too short.

When it is of satisfactory length, the horse is bridled as follows: The student stands close to the horse on the left side facing forward with the bridle in the left hand. The right arm is placed on the horse's neck so that the wrist rests at the poll area and the fingers extend down the forehead. The bridle is now raised in front of the horse's face so that the crownpiece is held in the right hand and the bit hangs squarely below the horse's mouth. The noseband can be held up out of the way with the right hand. In this position, with the right arm on the horse's neck, the student can exert downward pressure on the head and neck if the horse does not accept the bit and tries to raise his head beyond the student's reach. Cradle the bit in the fingers of the left hand while inserting the thumb in the interdental space on the left side of the mouth and exerting a downward pressure on the gum to cause the horse to open his mouth. As his mouth opens, the bit is slipped gently into place without hitting the teeth. The noseband is then lowered into place and the left hand

BILL CULBERTSON

Fig. 4. Proper bridling ensures the handler maximum control over the horse and helps prevent him from establishing bad habits.

moved to the crownpiece. The student's right hand is used to bend first the right ear and then the left ear carefully forward to assume their proper place in the bridle. The ears should never be bent backward against their natural cartilage structure, which gives them the curved-forward appearance (fig. 4).

The right ear should always be secured in place before the left so that the right side of the bridle is in place in case the horse becomes frightened or pulls away. If that should happen, the student can usually hold the left side of the bridle in place and move with the horse, thus preventing the horse from establishing a habit of jerking away during bridling.

When the bridle is adjusted to the proper fit, the bit rests comfortably with one wrinkle at each corner of the mouth. If the bit is too low, it will interfere with the teeth, and the pressure from the reins will be applied in improper places. Too tight a bit will make the horse look as though he were smiling, causing discomfort and possible head throwing. When an adjustment of the cheekpiece is made, it is best to adjust the cheekpiece on both sides to keep the bridle as even as possible on the horse's head. Lead the bridled horse by the reins in the same position used to lead the horse with a halter and rope.

Have the student visually recheck all the equipment and tighten the girth before mounting.

Tying a Horse—Safety Knots

A quick-release knot should always be used when tying a horse. This knot pulls free with a single tug if an emergency situation occurs.

Two common knots are the *clove hitch* (fig. 5) and the *manger tie* (fig. 6). While both knots are safe to use, the clove hitch is preferred in a school setting because it will not tighten so much that it cannot be released if a horse suddenly pulls back

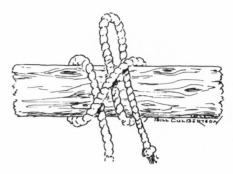

Fig. 5. The clove hitch.

against the rope. A manger tie can tighten against itself so that it is almost impossible to free it. If a horse becomes adept at pulling the quick-release knot free with his teeth, the end of the rope must be dropped through the loop to prevent the horse from untying himself.

It is important for students to remember to tie a horse at the height of his withers or slightly above. A horse should *never* be tied so low that he can get his foot over the rope when extending his head to the ground or so high that he cannot hold his head in a natural position.

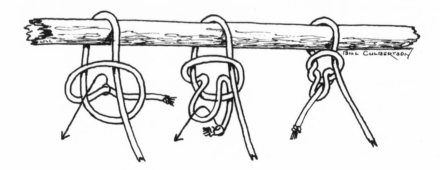

Fig. 6. The manger tie.

Chapter 2

Equipment

The student must become familiar with the correct names of the parts of the saddle and bridle (see Appendix A). Learning the correct terminology helps the student become more conscientious in caring for the equipment and encourages proper use of the horseman's vocabulary.

Care and Storage of Equipment

After use, a saddle and bridle should be cleaned and saddle-soaped before storage. The bit should be washed, and if the bridle is used on several horses, the bit should be dipped in a disinfectant to help prevent the spread of contagious agents. Liquid glycerin is a good soaping solution; it is easy to use, is readily absorbed, leaves little residue, and does not spot leather when used as directed. Neat's-foot oil should be applied to leather only as needed; if too much oil is used, it will rub off on the horse and rider and may dissolve the stitching on the equipment. Pure neat's-foot oil is generally preferred to a compound, because less oil is required for complete penetration, and no cloudy or hazy cast remains on the leather. General climatic conditions and the suppleness, or degree of dryness, of the leather are the indicators that should govern the oiling of equipment.

Cover the saddles and store them on a rack in a dry place; dampness is an enemy of leather, permeating the pores and destroying its texture. If a rack is not available, a saddle can be placed on a padded chairback, or it can be turned over on its seat and placed upside down on a soft material. The stirrups are dressed (run up) when the saddle is not in use.

Bridles are placed in a figure-eight position before they are hung on a bracket, allowing the crownpiece to remain in a natural open and rounded position, much as it appears on the horse's head. Placing a bridle in this position keeps the reins from hitting the ground—and indicates that its user cares about his equipment and has a measure of pride and air of professionalism about his work.

To figure-eight a bridle, hold it in the left hand and unbuckle the noseband. Lift the ends of the reins so that they rest in the hand by the crownpiece. Pick up the right side of the throatlatch, cross it over the front portion of the bridle toward the rear, and run it through the reins. The reins will now drop down and remain secure on the throatlatch. Continue around the bridle to the front, cross over the front of the bridle for the second time, and secure the leather piece in the two keepers on the left side of the throatlatch. The X formed by the throatlatch is now visible across the front of the bridle. Hang the bridle on the bracket and fasten the noseband completely around the head-stall and reins by running it through its leather keepers (fig. 7). Using the keepers instead of buckling the throatlatch and noseband enables the user to undo the figure eight with a minimum of time and effort.

Saddle pads, girth guards, and bounce pads should be aired, dried, and stored neatly in their designated places.

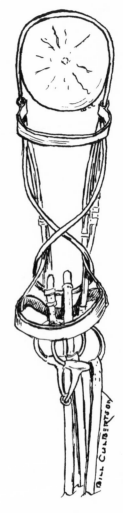

Fig. 7. When the bridle is not in use, keep it in the figure-eight position.

Chapter 3

Arena Activities for Beginners

Mount and Dismount

The instructor should demonstrate the proper way to mount and dismount or describe the procedure while another competent rider demonstrates. The explanation must be slow and methodical to ensure understanding. Explain that when the rider is mounting care must be taken not to jerk the horse's mouth with the reins. Explain that, if balance is lost, the rider should hold onto the saddle rather than try to regain balance by exerting pressure on the reins.

The mount and dismount should be practiced from both sides. While the horse is usually mounted from the left, emergency situations may make it necessary to mount or dismount from the right.

MOUNT

1. To mount, the rider stands close to the horse's left shoulder facing the rear at approximately a three-quarter angle (fig. 8).
2. The rider holds the reins in the left hand and maintains light contact with the horse's mouth. The left hand is placed on the horse's neck just in front of the withers.
3. The rider grasps the left stirrup with the right hand and inserts the left foot.
4. The rider moves the right hand to the cantle of the saddle.
5. The rider moves close to the horse's side so that the knee is pressed against the saddle and the toe is pressed into the girth. The rider springs off the ground and straight up beside the horse, adjusting the body weight over the saddle.
6. The rider's right leg swings clear of the horse's croup, and the right hand is moved from the cantle to the pommel of the saddle.
7. The rider settles gently into the saddle and places the right foot in the right stirrup.
8. The rider takes the reins in both hands.

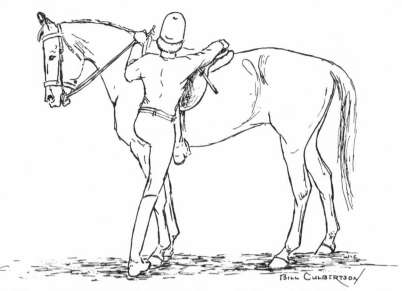

Fig. 8. When mounting, the rider stands close to the horse's left shoulder and faces the rear at approximately a three-quarter angle.

Fig. 9. When dismounting, the rider steps quietly to the ground.

DISMOUNT

1. The rider holds the reins in the left hand and places the left hand on the crest as positioned for the mount.
2. The rider places the right hand on the pommel while removing the right foot from the stirrup and swinging the right leg over the horse's croup.
3. The weight is transferred to the left stirrup, and then the rider removes the right hand from the pommel and places it on the cantle of the saddle.
4. Placing the toe of the left foot in the girth to prevent the horse from being gouged, the rider steps to the ground with the right foot. When dismounting, the rider should be standing in the same position used for mounting (fig. 9).
5. The rider moves the reins over the horse's head and holds them in the correct position to lead the horse.

VAULTING DISMOUNT

When using a vaulting dismount, a rider must always remove both feet from the stirrups before beginning the dismount (fig. 10). Emphasize that under no circumstance should a rider throw a leg over the withers to dismount; this position could cause a rider to strike the ground face first if the horse moved unexpectedly.

1. The rider moves the reins to the left hand and removes both feet from the stirrups.
2. The rider leans forward and places the left hand on the horse's neck and the right hand on the pommel.
3. Swinging the right leg over the horse's croup, the rider vaults (jumps) off, landing close to the horse on the left side in a position approximately next to the pommel of the saddle.
4. The rider moves the reins over the horse's head for leading.

Holding the Reins in Two Hands

An explanation of the way to hold the reins of a single-rein bridle should immediately follow the demonstration of mounting and dismounting.

With a single-rein bridle a rein is held in each hand, with the excess rein, called the *bight,* passing under the right rein and falling on the right side of the horse's neck. Each rein either comes below the little finger of the hand or passes between the little finger and the third finger. The rein then passes through the palm of the hand and over the index finger and is held in place by pressure of the thumb against the index finger.

Fig. 10. *When using the popular vaulting dismount, the rider must always remove both feet from the stirrups before beginning the dismount.*

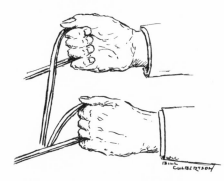

Fig. 11. *When using a snaffle bridle, hold one rein in each hand.*

How a Snaffle Bit Works

An explanation of the mechanics of a snaffle bit and the pressure points in a horse's mouth follows. Note that the jointed snaffle bit has a broken mouthpiece that exerts pressure primarily on the tongue and corners of the mouth when rein pressure is applied. The hinged mouthpiece allows the rider to exert pressure on one side of the bit without disturbing the other side and, in more advanced work, to apply different kinds of pressure simultaneously to maintain lateral bend and vertical flexion and to encourage lateral movements. The absence of a shank means that the snaffle bit does not operate on a leverage principle.

In an effort to understand a horse's behavior, it is important to remember that the larger and smoother the surface area of the bit the more evenly and gently the pressure is distributed in the mouth. A gentle bit with a large, round, smooth mouthpiece can allow the horse to concentrate on what the rider is asking him to do throughout his whole body, while a narrow, more severe mouthpiece can restrict the horse's attention to the uncomfortable action taking place in his mouth.

Work in a File

To ensure observance of safety measures and control of the horse, assemble the students in single-file formation approximately one horse's length apart. When students can maintain proper spacing and adequate control, they may space out on the rail and work individually within a group. Work in a file should resume at the introduction of each gait.

The following activities should be taught in the sequence in which they are presented.

Walk and Halt

Moving forward and halting the horse are the building blocks of riding. Just as in learning to drive a car, a student will feel more secure and relaxed when the horse will start and stop with ease.

The instructor begins by explaining the aids for the walk, noting that the reins must be loose enough to allow the horse to move forward. Constant attention must be given to this matter, for the beginner will have a tendency to balance with the reins rather than with the body. If this habit is allowed to develop, it not only causes the horse endless pain and discomfort but also prevents the rider from developing an independent seat, which is the basis of all equestrian skills.

The aids for the walk should be clearly explained as follows:

1. Loosen the reins enough for the horse to move forward freely.
2. Apply pressure with both lower legs at the girth. The action of the legs is the same as the action of the hand on the reins. It is a press-and-release action. Constant pressure should never be used; it would dull the horse's sides.

Halting in the initial stages is accomplished by having the student

1. Sit deep in the saddle.
2. Close hands on reins.
3. Release all pressure as the halt is completed. Use the work-in-a-file formation while the students practice the walk and halt. Precede each command with the phrase "Prepare to . . . ," which alerts the students to the coming command and gives them time to think about the aids they will apply. For example, the instructor says, "Prepare to halt," pauses a moment, and then says, "Halt."

School Movements

School movements help make basic learning more interesting and aid in teaching rider balance and control of the horse. In more advanced work these movements serve as suppling exercises for the horse and can be incorporated into simple drills that introduce the element of precision.

The basic school movements are *full turn, half-turn, cross-the-school, cross-the-diagonal,* and *up-the-centerline* (see Appendix B for diagrams of basic school movements). All school movements can be performed at a walk and trot. In advanced work cross-the-diagonal and half-turn movements require a simple change of lead when performed at the canter.

Basic school movements that do not require a change of direction are taught first because beginners can easily become confused by the amount of information they must assimilate and transmit into action in a relatively short period of time.

Positive reinforcement in the form of verbal encouragement is essential during this period. Phrases like "Yes, you can do it," "Good," "Let's try it again," and "Much better!" must play an important part in the instructor's teaching.

In implementing school movements, the instructor gives the command "Prepare to . . ." in sufficient time to allow the file to begin the movement at a designated point. Dressage letters are helpful markers when used to designate the centerline and bisect the long sides of the area for crossing the school. Full turns and half-turns should be large to allow for easy completion. When movements are being executed in file formation, each rider should turn the horse's head to the outside of the horse in front to maintain the proper spacing between horses.

Suppling Exercises

Muscles used in riding cannot be readily strengthened while the rider is dismounted. For this reason exercises to develop strength, pliancy, and control of the parts of the body are an essential part of all equitation activities. Exercises are introduced at a walk and then performed at a trot and canter, depending on the rider's level of proficiency. While the canter is the most favorable gait for suppling the rider's loins, the trot is the most useful gait for developing muscles. Care should be taken when introducing exercises at the trot, for fatigue comes quickly. If work beyond this point continues, the insufficient muscles will retard progress. Begin each lesson with short exercise periods. Students start work on the rail, with each rider tying a knot in the reins to keep them short enough to maintain control by carrying them in the outside hand.

To help combat rigidity and obtain maximum relaxation of the muscles, exercises should be performed systematically, beginning with the head and neck and working down to the ankles and feet. Each exercise should be repeated five or six times in both directions.

SUPPLING THE NECK

The rider turns the head and eyes as far as possible to the right, keeping the upper body in the proper position. The exercise is then repeated to the left. Next the head is brought upward and backward as far as possible, then forward and downward (fig. 12).

SUPPLING THE SHOULDERS

The rider's arm is extended straight up, the palm of the hand facing forward. The

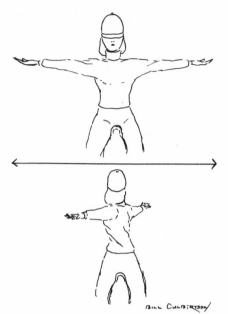

Fig. 14. The "up-out-pivot-pivot" exercise supples the waist and loin.

Fig. 12. Head rotations help supple the neck.

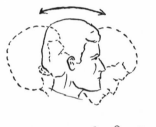

arm is then rotated backward until it has subscribed a full circle (fig. 13). Since the rider is encouraged to "open the shoulders," the shoulder is always rotated backward to aid in the development of the correct shoulder position. Each arm and shoulder are rotated individually and then together. The canter is the best gait to use when performing this exercise, but only when the rider has developed sufficient balance and control.

SUPPLING THE WAIST AND LOIN

With a knot tied in the reins and the reins lying on the horse's neck, the rider extends both arms straight upward and then brings them on a horizontal plane with the shoulders. Maintaining this position, the rider turns the head, neck, and eyes to the right toward the horse's tail and pivots to the left (fig. 14). The rider actually "twists" the upper body, suppling the waist and loins while

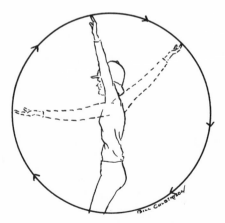

Fig. 13. Suppling the shoulders. Shoulder rotations are always executed in a backward motion.

turning the head, neck, and eyes. The rotation of the arms and shoulders supples the corresponding parts of the body. The exercise is correctly performed only when the rider's seat remains firmly in the saddle and the legs remain in their correct position. This "up-out-pivot-pivot" exercise should be performed at all gaits as the rider becomes able. The exercise also encourages the rider to maintain a deep seat and proper leg position.

In another exercise to supple the loins, the rider rotates the upper body and carries the right hand across the reins and downward so that it is in a position opposite the horse's left shoulder. After stroking the shoulder several times, the rider repeats the exercise in the opposite direction, the left hand being placed on the horse's right shoulder (fig. 15).

In a variation of this exercise the rider touches the horse's left shoulder as described above and then extends the right arm backward to touch the horse's right haunch. The reins are then switched to the right hand, and the exercise is repeated in the opposite direction, left hand to the horse's right shoulder, then backward to the left haunch.

The following exercise is usually performed at a halt, but with care can be executed at a walk. The rider bends forward, keeping the lower leg underneath, and touches the chin to the horse's crest. The rider then straightens the upper body, leans backward, and rests the head and shoulders on the horse's croup (fig. 16). The hands must not be used to support this movement, nor should the rider's legs be moved from their correct position.

SUPPLING THE KNEE

The rider removes either foot from the stirrup and carries the leg slightly away from the horse. The leg is then carried backward and upward until it is on a

Bill Culbertson

Fig. 15. Touching the horse's shoulder and then the opposite haunch also supples the waist and loin.

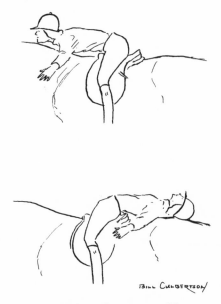

Bill Culbertson

Fig. 16. Suppling the waist and loin. During this exercise the leg must remain under the body. The hands are not used for support.

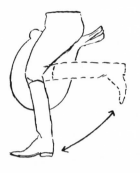

Bill Culbertson

Fig. 17. To supple the knee, carry the leg backward and upward until it is on a horizontal plane with the knee joint.

horizontal plane with the knee joint (fig. 17). Without pause the leg is returned to its normal position. This exercise should be performed several times, the rider alternating the position with each leg.

SUPPLING THE ANKLE

The rider removes each foot from the

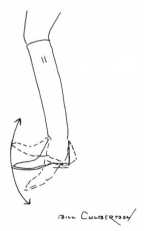

Bill Culbertson

Fig. 18. To remove stiffness from the ankles, rotate each ankle individually outward in a circular motion.

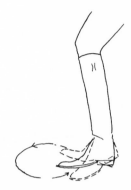

Bill Culbertson

Fig. 19. Suppling the ankle. Flexing the toe upward and then downward helps remove stiffness.

stirrup and flexes the toes upward as far as possible and then extends them downward as far as possible (fig. 18). The exercise should be repeated several times with each foot.

Following this exercise the rider rotates each ankle individually. The right ankle should be rotated in a clockwise movement, the toe of the right foot subscribing a circle to the right on a horizontal plane with the ground (fig. 19). The left ankle is then rotated in a counterclockwise movement, the left toe subscribing the same circular movement.

Introducing the Trot

The trot should be introduced as a two-beat diagonal gait with the footfall sequence explained (fig. 20). Once the students understand the footfall pattern —the left forefoot and the right hind foot moving together and the right forefoot and the left hind foot moving together —they will be able to grasp the concept of the rising trot and the proper use of diagonals.

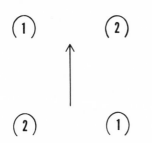

Fig. 20. Footfall sequence for the trot, a two-beat diagonal gait.

AIDS

In this session the student should be introduced only to the *feel* of the trot and not be bothered with the diagonals. The aids for the trot should be explained as follows:

1. Hold the hands low, one on each side of the horse's neck and just in front of the withers. Care should be taken not to pull back on the reins unintentionally.
2. Apply pressure simultaneously with both lower legs positioned at the girth, to move forward.

LESSON PROCEDURE

Demonstrate the trot and ask the students to note the following characteristics of correct body position:

1. Erect but relaxed upper body.
2. Shoulders open and rotated slightly to the rear.
3. Arms carried close to the body with elbows bent and close to rider's sides.
4. Weight on the sitting bones to help keep the seat in the saddle.
5. The lower leg positioned under the rider's body.
6. The weight directed toward the ground through a lowered heel position.

Assemble the students in file formation. Ask the first rider in the file to name the aids for a trot, and, when they are named correctly, execute a trot to the end of the file. The instructor says: "First person in the file, what are the aids for the trot?" Answer: "Prepare to trot to the end of the file"—pause—"and trot to the end of the file." This procedure is continued until all the students have trotted to the end of the file at least twice.

The third time the first person in the file may be asked to trot, walk, and then trot on the end of the file. Using this pattern for variety, the instructor says: "First person in the file, prepare for trot" —pause—"and trot"—pause—"prepare to walk"—"and walk"—"Good!" or "Let's try it again" (emphasize encouragement and praise) "and trot on to the end of the file." The instructor should be certain that all students drop to a walk for several steps before rejoining the file to ensure control and to keep horses from running back to a group.

A pattern such as walk-trot-full turn-trot-halt-walk is an excellent method to use to evaluate the students' understanding and control of the material presented.

Introducing the Rising Trot (Posting)

In explaining the rising trot, refer to the previous discussion of the trot as a two-beat gait with the diagonal pairs of legs moving together. With this explanation it will be easy for students to see why a one-, two-beat gait readily lends itself to a rising and sitting, or one-two, up-down movement of the rider.

That is enough information for a beginner to digest at this point. A discussion of diagonals should follow *only* when a rider can execute a rising trot with fair control. If the rising trot and diagonals are introduced at the same time, fatigue and frustration will result. *Note: Since beginners will have a tendency to balance with their reins, ask them to tie a knot in their reins and carry them loosely in their outside hand until the rising trot is stabilized. This prevents the horse from being hit in the mouth and forces the student to use his body in an effort to develop an independent seat.*

LESSON PROCEDURE

Demonstrate the rising trot, tying a knot in the reins and carrying them in the outside hand. Have the students note that the upper body is inclined slightly forward in the rising trot and that the rising motion is generated from the rider's knees and thighs, *not* executed by pumping off the stirrups with the feet. The lower leg should stay under the rider's body and on the horse.

Reestablishing file formation, the instructor asks the first person in the file to explain the aids for the trot, and, when they are said correctly, to execute a rising trot to the end of the file.

During this time the instructor calls "up-down" or "one-two" to assist the student in understanding the desired movement. The student should say "up-down" or "one-two" with the instructor.

Each person in the file should trot-rising to the end of the file at least twice. If no problems occur, the file as a whole may trot. The instructor says, "File, prepare for rising trot"—pause—and "File, rising trot." When the file can execute a rising trot, a series of movements such as walk-halt-rising trot-walk-halt may follow. If this exercise is performed with control, the file may execute large basic school movements at the rising trot.

The above material and exercises are designed to acquaint the students with the basic movement and feel of the trot. Once this has been achieved, present a discussion of the need to use the proper diagonals. This discussion should include the following points:

Explanation of Diagonals

When traveling on the rail in the arena or when working on a curved line, the rider rises when the horse's outside

Fig. 21. To post on the correct diagonal, the rider rises as the horse's outside shoulder moves forward.

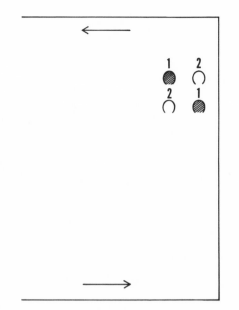

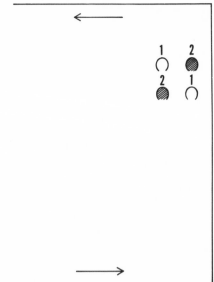

Fig. 22. The rising diagonal, working on the left rein. The rider rises when the outside (right) fore and inside (left) hind feet are moving off the ground and the inside (left) fore and outside (right) hind feet are on the ground.

Fig. 23. The sitting diagonal, working on the left rein. The rider sits when the outside fore (right) and inside hind (left) feet are on the ground and the inside fore (left) and outside hind (right) feet are off the ground. The rider rises and sits on the same diagonal pair of legs.

shoulder moves forward. This is referred to as "rising on the outside diagonal" (fig. 21). Since a rider rises and sits on the same diagonal pair of legs as it leaves and returns to the ground, it is important that the rider change the diagonal—that is, rise and sit on the other diagonal pair of legs—whenever a change of direction occurs to ensure even muscle development in the horse. If a rider always rises and sits on the same diagonal pair of legs, the horse will become one-sided, over-developing one diagonal set of muscles at the expense of the other. When this problem arises, it becomes difficult to straighten the horse, the horse tires more quickly, and the rhythm of the gait is eventually destroyed.

THE CORRECT AIDS AND THEIR DRIVING FORCE

A rider executes a rising trot on the left rein (rider's left hand toward the center of the arena). The rider rises as the horse's outside shoulder moves forward (right fore and left hind off the ground, left fore and right hind on the ground). As the rider sits, the inside hind leg is on the ground (fig. 22). This is the driving leg and the one that must reach the farthest under the horse's body when he is working on a bend or circle. It therefore becomes the weight-bearing leg. Since in their most effective use the rider's driving aids usually coincide with the seat returning to the saddle, the rider can

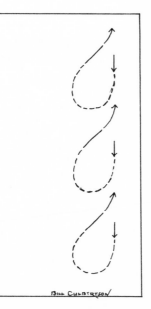

Fig. 24. When performing the half-turn, the rider remains between the horse working in front and the horse working behind. As in the full turn, the half-turn is large enough to allow the rider to plan the maneuver and maintain the tempo.

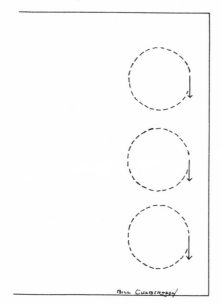

Fig. 25. When executing an individual full turn on the rail, the rider remains between the horse working in front and the horse working behind.

influence the driving or inside leg most effectively when the seat is in the saddle and the rider can generate an extra measure of impulsion by squeezing with the legs. Since the rider sits and squeezes with the legs when the horse's inside hind leg is on the ground, the impulsion the rider generates will result in a longer-reaching stride, for the rider's weight comes off the inside hind leg as it reaches under the horse's body and the rider rises on the outside diagonal (fig. 23).

When working in the open, encourage the rider to change the diagonal every five or ten minutes to ensure even muscle development and prevent one-sidedness in the horse.

Follow with practice sessions having the students use the proper diagonals traveling on the left and right rein. To change the diagonal while trotting, the student sits one extra beat and rises on the following beat. The instructor can help each student by counting "one-two" until the rider can look at the horse's outside shoulder and properly coordinate movement with it. Keep work sessions to a moderate length; students will tire mentally and physically from the exertion. Vary the work and walk on a long rein to keep students relaxed and willing.

ARENA EXERCISES AND
INDIVIDUAL WORK ON THE RAIL

Sufficient material is now available with which to vary the lessons; initiate simple, safe games; and present a modified walk-trot show class. First, work students individually on the rail at a walk, a sitting trot, and a rising trot. When sufficient control through walk-trot-walk-halt has been determined by the instructor, riders are asked to half-turn and full-turn individually at a walk and then at a trot (figs. 24 and 25). When the exercise is executed correctly, the rider remains

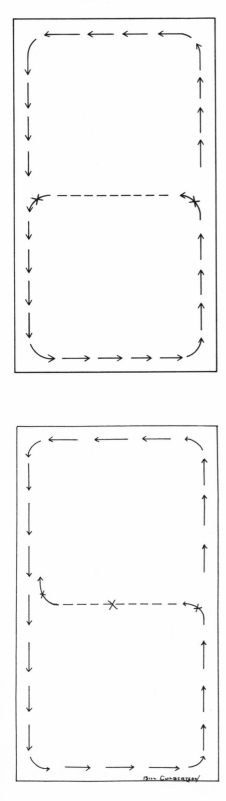

Fig. 26. Cross-the-school.

between the horse working in front and the one behind. The exercise encourages the rider to look in the direction of travel. It is therefore an excellent test of control and forces the rider to concentrate and plan the maneuver being performed. The instructor may also ask a student by name to cross the school. If all the riders are working on the left rein, the student asked to perform the maneuver simply looks up; crosses the school, maintaining a straight line from point to point; and continues on the same rein (fig. 26). This exercise should be performed in both directions at a trot.

A variation of the cross-the-school exercise can be employed when the rider has performed the basic maneuver without incident. Using the variation, a student is asked to "cross the school and change the rein." This exercise requires the rider to cross the school, change the diagonal at the center point, change the rein upon reaching the opposite long side, and work to the inside of the riders on the rail who have not yet been called to perform (fig. 27).

The same exercise can be executed across the diagonal. When tracking right, a student is asked to cross the diagonal at *M* (for example) and change the rein (fig. 28). For instance, the instructor would say to a student, "Kathy, when you reach *M*, cross the diagonal and change the rein and work to the inside of the other riders."

In this exercise the rider must ride *through* a corner, ride a straight line from letter to letter or marker to marker, change the diagonal at the center point, change the rein at *K* (for example), and work to the inside of the group. Even-

Fig. 27. Cross-the-school and change-the-rein.

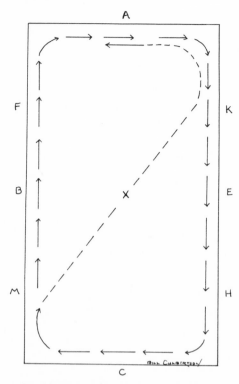

A

F

B

M

K

E

H

X

C

BILL CULBERTSON

Fig. 28. Cross-the-diagonal and change-the-rein.

The walk-trot class consists of rail work with an emphasis on smoothness and control. Any combination of walk-trot-halt movements may be used. Riders are asked to dismount and mount individually. Ties are decided by asking for individual work, such as trotting a full turn or a half-turn with a change of diagonal.

In addition to serving as a change of pace, such activity introduces an atmosphere of competition that can be a great motivating force among students. Ribbons can be awarded through fifth place.

Elementary Drill Work

Simple drills are an exciting and easy way to stimulate students to think and respond quickly to a given situation. To begin a drill, each student selects a partner. Horses are paired as evenly matched in stride as possible. Let a fairly well moving pair lead the drill. Riders actually ride in double-file formation, remaining a horse's length apart throughout the maneuver. Horses in a pair should be head to head, and the riders in each pair should remain stirrup to stirrup. To maintain proper spacing during a turn, a pair of students rides slightly to the outside of the pair in front (fig. 29). When turning, it will be necessary for the inside horse to slow down and for the outside horse to speed up since it will have to cover a little more ground.

The instructor uses the phrases "Drill, prepare to . . ." (full turn) and, "Drill, . . ." (full turn). Announce each maneuver in sufficient time to allow the drill to negotiate the command smoothly and at the proper place in the arena. All drill movements are performed in a large pattern to allow for steady rhythm and even tempo. A simple drill may be performed with the following commands:

tually a total change of direction of all riders will be accomplished. At a trot the cross-the-diagonal-and-change-the-rein exercise provides the beginning rider with a mental and physical challenge.

Walk-Trot Show Class

Initiating a walk-trot show class is an excellent way to add variety and color to beginning equitation activities. American Horse Shows Association (AHSA) rules, which pertain to English equitation and breed pleasure classes, should be followed. A knowledgeable individual not associated with the equitation class should serve as the judge. Give each student a number and follow horse-show protocol as closely as possible.

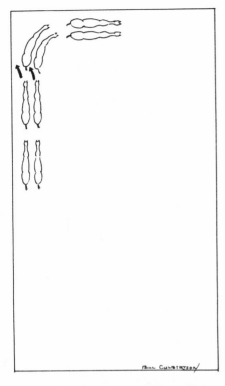

Fig. 29. *To maintain proper spacing,
when making a turn each pair of riders
turns slightly to the outside of the pair
of riders in front.*

able, it will greatly increase the quality of
the event. Keep the length of drill between
five and seven minutes for beginners.

Introducing the Canter

In introducing the canter, it is important
to remember that beginners will think of
the canter as a "faster" gait and will
naturally have some apprehension. For
this reason the purpose of the session must
be to help the students understand the
motion and feel of the canter. Leads are
not explained until riders can ask for a
canter, obtain it, and remain adequately
balanced and in control of the horse.
Once the apprehension dissipates, the
rider will relax and enjoy the smoothness
of this three-beat gait.

Encourage the students to become
familiar with the footfall sequence of the
canter. At this time it is sufficient for the
instructor to point out that the outside
hind leg initiates the canter departure and
is the first beat of the three-beat sequence;
the inside hind leg and outside foreleg are
the diagonal pair of legs that follow; and,
last, the inside foreleg reaches out and
completes the footfall pattern (figs. 30
and 31).

1. Riders, track left on the rail at a rising
   trot.
2. Up the centerline.
3. Track right at the opposite end.
4. Cross the school.
5. Full turn.
6. Up the centerline.
7. Track left.
8. Cross the diagonal (automatic change
   of rein).
9. Cross the following diagonal (automatic change of rein).
10. Halt through the walk.

An active imagination can produce a
variety of simple drills. If music is avail-

Fig. 30. *Footfall sequence, canter right lead.*

Fig. 31. *Footfall sequence, canter left lead.*

AIDS

The aids for the canter are as follows:

1. The rider's hands are held low, one on each side of the horse's neck and just in front of the withers. The rider must take care to avoid an unintentional backward pull on the reins during the canter departure and during the canter itself.
2. The rider slightly shortens the inside rein so that the horse is looking in the direction of travel. When the rider can see the outside corner of the horse's inside eye, sufficient bend has been obtained.
3. The rider places the inside leg at the girth and sits slightly inward, lowering the knee and heel.
4. The rider places the outside leg approximately four inches behind the girth.
5. The rider applies pressure with *both* legs to pick up the horse and place him in a canter.

The instructor must watch carefully to see that students use *both legs* to initiate the canter departure. The reason for this becomes apparent in more advanced work, when the rider's inside leg is used to maintain a bend in the horse working on a circular tract, while the outside leg becomes dominant when a rider executes a flying change.

LESSON PROCEDURE

When working with a beginner, tie a knot in the reins and have the student hold the reins in the outside hand during the first few canter departures. Using this method, students will quickly find their own balance and will not rely on the reins for support. As students relax and give the aids properly, the reins may be taken in both hands.

If a rider's hands are unsteady, the rider should place one hand on each side of the horses's neck so as not to apply unintentional pressure to the horse's mouth. Alternate methods of keeping the hands quiet and steady include holding onto the front of the saddle pad on each side of the saddle or placing a hand on each side of the pommel. These hand positions are considered only temporary aids to teach the student the feel of quiet hands. Once the student understands the feel of quiet hands, the hands should be removed from that position and carried in the correct manner.

The instructor next demonstrates the correct position of the rider in the saddle at the canter, sitting firmly on the sitting bones and not pitching forward onto the crotch. The upper body is carried erect, the legs remaining under the rider with each calf in light contact with the horse's sides. The head must be up, the rider looking in the direction of travel. Hands are quiet and steady as they are secured on either side of the pommel. Have the students execute downward transitions through the trot, to the walk, to a smooth halt.

Assemble mounted students in file formation and ask the first person in the file to give the aids for the canter, and pick up a few strides of a sitting trot, and then canter to the end of the file. The instructor calls out the name of the first person in the file and says, "What are the aids for the canter?"—answer— "Prepare to canter to the end of the file" —pause—"and canter to the end of the file." This procedure is continued until all the students have gained a measure of confidence and balance. The instructor can make individual comments as each student canters to the end of the file.

Introducing the canter may require as many as three sessions depending entirely on the ability and experience of the students. As a measure of control becomes evident, the first rider in the file may be asked to execute a simple pattern, such as trot rising-trot sitting-canter-trot-full turn-and-walk to the end of the file.

Note: Point out to students that a canter is performed after a few strides of the sitting trot if the rider is executing a rising trot when the "prepare to canter" command is given.

The instructor must continue to reinforce students' actions with positive comments of encouragement and praise. The expression on each student's face and the body position and balance will provide an astute instructor with all the information needed regarding the rider's mental attitude and degree of physical ease.

Distinguishing Leads

When students are able to canter with control, it is time for a discussion on the importance of leads. Incorporate the following material into a presentation along with a basic demonstration.

At a canter or gallop the horse will extend a foreleg and hind leg *on the same side* farther ahead than the foreleg and hind leg on the other side. The foreleg and hind leg on the same side that attain this more forward position are called the *leading legs* or, more commonly, the *lead* (fig. 32).

At the canter the leading foreleg is the final, or third, beat of the footfall sequence. When a horse is traveling to the left or on a circle to the left, he should be on the left lead, the left fore and hind leg moving in a more advanced position than the right fore and hind leg (fig. 33).

If a horse is traveling to the right or on a circle to the right, he should be on the right lead, the right fore and hind leg

Fig. 32. *If a horse is cantering on the correct lead on a circular track, the inside fore and hind legs travel in a more advanced position than that of the outside fore and hind legs.*

Fig. 33. *Left lead.*

Fig. 34. Right lead.

assuming a more advanced position than the left (fig. 34). If a horse is positioned to canter a circle to the right and begins the circle on the incorrect or wrong lead —in this case the left lead—his movement will be unbalanced. In such a case a horse will usually try to remedy the situation himself by breaking to a trot and then assuming the correct lead or by trying to change leads without breaking gait, which for an unskilled horse and rider can result in stumbling or falling.

UNMOUNTED DEMONSTRATION

A very simple and effective method of demonstrating leads and their relationship to proper movement is to ask a student to get a broomstick and put it between the legs like a stick horse. Now ask the student to canter. Whichever leg extends farther will be the lead. To demonstrate the importance of being on

the correct lead, ask the student to canter on the left lead and then to maintain the left lead while cantering a circle to the right. The difficulty the student will have, opposed to the simplicity of cantering a circle to the right, will clearly illustrate how ability to move in the direction of travel is enhanced or impaired depending on the correctness or incorrectness of the footfall sequence.

MOUNTED DEMONSTRATION

Students will be better able to visualize a lead and its importance if two matching leg wraps are placed on a horse's left fore and left hind legs. Canter the horse in a circle to the left. The leg wraps will enable students to see the left fore and hind leg moving in a more advanced position than the right fore and hind legs. Next canter the horse in a circle to the right and have the students note the more advanced position attained by the right fore and hind legs, the legs without the leg wraps. Finally, canter a circle on the wrong lead so that students can observe the problem of balance encountered by both horse and rider.

A horse without leg wraps can now be used to demonstrate circles to the left and right and can also be used on the rail to give students an opportunity to determine the lead on which the horse is working.

PRACTICE IN FILE FORMATION

The students should now be able to identify visually a horse traveling on the proper lead. Have them return to file formation on the rail and practice applying the correct aids to obtain the desired lead. The reins should be held correctly in two hands. Tracking left just before a corner can encourage correct bend and lead. Ask the first person in the file to

1. Prepare for a few steps of sitting trot —pause—and sitting trot.
2. Turn the horse's head *slightly* in the direction of travel so that *only* the outside corner of the inside eye is visible to the rider. *Note: The rider will tend to overbend the horse's head and neck in the direction of travel. This problem is easily corrected if the student maintains sufficient contact on the outside rein to limit the bend and prevent the horse's neck and head from being overbent to the inside. The word "slightly" in this instance means about one inch so that the horse will be looking where he is going and have his body positioned properly to canter on the correct lead.*
3. Apply the correct aids for the canter.
4. Canter.
5. Visually check the lead for correctness by looking to see that the horse's inside shoulder is moving in a more forward position than that of the outside shoulder.

When all the riders have performed this exercise tracking left, the instructor calls for a half-turn and repeats the exercise tracking right. When sufficient progress has been made, the instructor may vary the exercise by asking the first person in the file for a sitting trot-canter-rising trot-walk-and-halt.

Rail Work at the Canter

Students may now work individually on the rail at the three basic gaits. When riders have shown adequate proficiency to canter on the correct lead with control, the instructor may ask each student individually to work to the inside of the rail and execute a full turn at the canter. *Note: The instructor must be certain that each horse is traveling on the correct lead before this exercise is performed.*

Give the students the following instructions before the exercise begins:

1. Ride a very large full turn. *Note: The natural tendency for beginning riders is to throw their weight to the inside when executing a circle. The horse then naturally moves under the rider's weight to compensate for the action, and the circle becomes so small that the horse is unbalanced and often breaks to a trot.*
2. Look up and in the direction of travel (this action helps put the rider's body in the proper position).
3. Maintain the aids for a canter throughout the full turn.

The Rein-Back

The footfall sequence for a horse moving backward is identical to the footfall sequence of a trot, the legs moving in diagonal pairs (fig. 35). Either pair of diagonal legs may initiate the movement, the second diagonal pair completing the

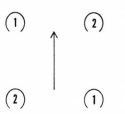

Fig. 35. *The footfall sequence of a horse trotting (above) and a horse backing (below) is identical; only the direction is different.*

footfall sequence. The only difference in the movement between the trot and the back is in the direction of travel.

When asking a horse to back from a halt, the rider must first position the horse correctly by asking for a slight *forward* movement. Usually a half-step or one full step of forward motion is sufficient to round the horse's body and position his legs up under his body so that he can pick up and place his diagonal pairs of legs without being pulled backward with his legs resisting the movement. *Note: It must be remembered that a horse must be in motion before he can execute a maneuver.*

The common faults—a high head, open mouth, hollow back, and lagging backward motion of the legs—are the result of lack of motion and excessive hand, bit, and rein action during the backing procedure.

AIDS

From a halt, ask the students to back their horses using the following procedure:

1. Sit erect in the saddle with the weight evenly distributed on both sitting bones and both lower legs resting lightly against the sides of the horse. The reins must be even to exert the same pressure on both sides of the mouth. Correct posture of the rider will encourage the horse to back in a straight line.
2. Obtain a few steps of forward movement. Dwell.
3. Squeeze one rein and then the other, alternating the rein pressure to communicate to the horse that backward movement is desired.
4. Apply pressure with both legs simultaneously at the girth in a press-and-release action to maintain the backward movement designated by the hand and reins.
5. Maintain *light* contact with the mouth, using a squeezing action on one rein and then the other, but *always use more leg than hand* to continue the backward motion. If the horse takes a few steps backward, halts, and refuses to continue backward, move the horse forward and start the process again.
6. If the horse deviates from backing in a straight line by swinging the haunches to the side, the rider should place the leg behind the girth and push the haunches back over so that the horse's body is again moving on a straight line. For example, if the horse swings his haunches to the right, the rider's right leg should be placed behind the girth on the right side of the horse and pressure applied to push the haunches back on a straight line. If the horse swings his haunches to the left, the rider uses the left leg behind the girth to correct the position and move the haunches back over on a straight line.

7. After four or five straight steps backward, the backing signal from the reins is discontinued and the horse is moved forward from the rider's legs.

Summary

At this point in the sequence of lessons each rider should have mastered safe, basic horse-handling procedures; should understand the footfall sequence of the walk, trot, canter, and back; and should be able to ride the three basic gaits with control while exhibiting good basic equitation skills. When these elements of equitation have been achieved, a rider should be advanced to the intermediate level.

Part Two

Intermediate
Equitation

Chapter 4

Body Language

At the intermediate level students should begin to develop a feel for riding and become able to elicit more response from the horse through the proper use of aids. Good communication through the use of "body language" develops the end result of a harmonious performance.

Body language is the method of communication used to telegraph the desires to the horse through the use of the rider's body (back, legs, sitting bones, and so on). Using this method of communication, the rider is able to execute the desired movements smoothly without depending solely on the reins for control and direction.

Part Two of this book examines the rider's body language, or basic methods in body communication. It details the points that must be understood and utilized until the rider is able to establish control, pace, and tempo through mental and muscular coordination.

Elements of Body Language

The following elements comprise the communication system of body language. Each element should be thought of as a link in a communication chain. If one link is weak or missing, the chain of communication from rider to mount is incomplete and limits the horse's ability to respond correctly. Students must study each element and work to combine the elements of body language with the basic aids for each gait presented in Part One.

WEIGHT

A rider's weight is one of the most valuable aids at his disposal. The position of the rider (too far forward, too far back, or too far to the inside or outside) greatly influences the horse's behavior and ability to perform. Two examples may be used to illustrate to students the necessity for proper weight control and balance:

Example 1. A person carrying a child on the back remains comfortable providing the child is centered and balanced in the correct position. If the child begins to slide downward or to lean off to one side, it is the natural tendency for the carrier to move under the child's weight to try to compensate for the change in weight distribution. A horse reacts in the same manner. If the rider's weight is inclined in one direction, *it is a natural tendency for the horse to move under the rider's weight.*

Example 2. Ask a student to stand in front of another student. Both students face the same direction. Ask the student standing behind (student B) to place the left arm on the other's left shoulder and the right arm on the other's right shoulder. Student A represents the horse; student B represents the rider. Student B now exerts pressure first on one shoulder and then on the other. Sufficient pressure will cause the shoulders of student A to become uneven, for the change in weight directly affects the level position of the shoulders. Through this demonstration students should more clearly understand how the position of weight can affect the balance of the horse.

This experiment can be taken one step further by asking student B to exert pressure on one shoulder and simultaneously gently pull student A's hair (representing the reins) in the opposite direction. All of a sudden the "horse" is being influenced with opposing aids, making it very difficult for him to know which way to turn. This simple experiment emphasizes that *the rider's weight and rein influences should always be in the same direction.* Unintentional use of opposing aids will result in confusion for both the horse and rider.

BACK

When the horse is moving forward, the rider's back remains relaxed, the small

of the back acting as a shock absorber. If the rider is tense, the back characterizes this tenseness by appearing too straight and rigid. Tenseness will also be present in the shoulders, and the rider will bounce in the saddle, unable to go with the motion of the horse.

A relaxed body moving rhythmically with the horse's motion communicates to the horse that everything is fine, and the horse will move ahead willingly. If a rider's back is relaxed to a lesser degree or is braced, the horse will feel the rider stop the motion in his back and respond to this aid by slowing his gait or executing a halt, depending on the degree to which the rider stops his own body action. A relaxed back is a "go" signal to the horse. Bracing of the back acts as a "slow down" or "halt" signal. The results derived from the proper use of the back are evident during the halt and half-halt.

In all situations the rider's torso should be elevated, the front line rounded, elbows carried by the sides, shoulder blades rotated backward with shoulder blades together and weight pushed downward to the heel. The head should be up with the eyes looking in the direction of travel.

SEAT

The seat serves as the rider's supporting surface. Through the seat sitting-bone influence is exerted on the horse. A change in weight distribution from front to back or to the side allows the rider to sit in common equilibrium (balance) with the horse's movements. A rider must learn to sit firmly but in a relaxed manner, without squeezing the lower legs to maintain balance. To aid them in developing an independent seat, longe students as frequently as possible.

SITTING BONES

The sitting bones are the two pelvic bones that can be felt through the gluteus maximus muscle when one is firmly seated on a hard surface (thin persons are more likely to be aware of sitting on their sitting bones than are individuals who have more natural padding in that area).

To demonstrate the location of sitting bones, the instructor asks students to sit firmly on a hard chair and distribute their weight evenly on both sitting bones. Then ask them to rock back and forth from one sitting bone to the other without disturbing the upright position of the upper body. Once mounted, riders must be able to adjust their weight from one sitting bone to the other or to distribute weight evenly on both sitting bones without collapsing a hip and leaning the upper body in the direction of travel. Collapsing a hip and leaning with the upper body are serious riding faults; they cause the horse to carry an unbalanced burden.

Sitting-bone influence is used in all movements. When riding a straight line, the rider should sit with the weight evenly distributed on both sitting bones. When executing a half-turn or full turn or when performing a movement on a single track requiring a bend, the rider adjusts more weight to the sitting bone in the direction of travel. For example, when the rider is on a circular track to the right, the right sitting bone bears more weight than the left. If the movement is being executed on the left rein, the left sitting bone bears more of the rider's weight. It is important for students to realize that large school movements require less differentiation in sitting-bone influence than do small figures. The smaller the figure the more a rider must influence the horse's movement by placing sufficient weight on the sitting bone in the direction of travel.

In discovering sitting-bone influence, riders often use too much influence and find their horses performing a circle smaller than the one intended. It is the instructor's responsibility to see that students do not overemphasize the use of sitting-bone influence and continue to maintain an erect upper body throughout the movement. Learning to ride a circle is very difficult, and students must be given sufficient time and practice sessions to allow them to "feel" exactly how much sitting-bone influence is enough for the size of the circle or movement being performed.

Effective use of sitting bones and proper position of the rider's lower leg when working on a circular track are interrelated topics for discussion. These two aids, along with proper positioning of the hands, allow the horse to bend and maintain a desired shape.

THIGH, KNEE, AND LOWER LEG

The thigh and knee must remain relaxed, flat, and steady against the saddle. The kneecap should always point forward (fig. 36). The inside of the lower leg—

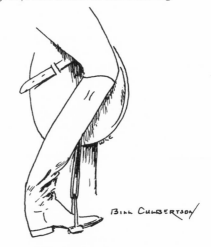

Fig. 36. *The thigh and knee remain flat against the saddle with the kneecap pointed forward. If excess flesh prevents the thigh from lying in the correct position, the rider grasps the back of the thigh and adjusts the excess flesh to the rear.*

not the back of the calf—remains in light contact with the horse's sides and influence his movement. The rider's leg exhibits a lowered heel, because when the heel is lowered, the knee on the same side is correspondingly lowered, making the calf muscles firm and strong. While riding a straight line or executing a half-halt or halt, the lower leg is positioned behind the girth to generate impulsion from the hindquarters.

When asking a horse to move forward and execute a bend, the rider places the inside leg at the girth and the outside leg approximately four inches behind the girth. Pressure from the inside leg bends the horse and also acts to support the horse's bending movement. The outside leg behind the girth prevents the hindquarters from falling out of the circular movement being performed.

For a rider to use the lower leg effectively, the leg must hang long, the calf remaining in light contact with the horse's side. In this position the leg can be used to ask the horse immediately to move forward, backward, or sideways, to slow down, or to halt. Common rider errors are squeezing with the thigh and pinching in with the knee to maintain balance or drawing the knee up and pulling the lower leg backward.

To correct lower-leg position, the entire leg must be moved back from the hip, not just from the knee. At all times the rider's leg must remain under the body; a leg placed too far backward or too far forward is detrimental to the rider's balance and control of the horse.

LESSON PROCEDURE

Using large school movements (circles, half-turns and half-turns in reverse), have each student practice turning and bending the horse through the use of sitting-bone and lower-leg influence. To turn left or to make a circle to the left,

the rider applies pressure with the left leg at the girth and the right leg behind the girth (fig. 37). Sufficient weight is placed on the left sitting bone, and the inside (left) rein is shortened so that the rider can see the outside corner of the horse's inside (left) eye, while the outside (right) rein is slightly lengthened to allow the horse to bend in the direction of travel. These combined aids are maintained until the rider leaves the circle and rides on to a straight line.

When the rider is moving in any straight line (crossing the diagonal, crossing the school, or traveling down the centerline), the rider's body must be positioned on the line being ridden with weight evenly distributed on both sitting bones (fig. 38). Both lower legs remain at the girth, while even, light rein contact is maintained on the bit. Using the body,

Bill Culbertson

Fig. 37. There must be coordination of hand, leg, and sitting-bone influence if the horse is to learn to turn and bend correctly.

BILL CULBERTSON

Fig. 38. When riding a straight line, the rider must clearly communicate this message to the horse by positioning his own body on a straight line and applying equal aid emphasis (hand, leg, and sitting bone) to both sides of the horse's body.

the rider is saying to the horse, "Now we are going straight."

ARENA EXERCISES

All arena exercises utilizing school movements are executed smoothly. Encourage the riders to *think ahead* and give their horses time to turn so that a movement can be performed at a given point. The use of letters or cones to mark the various points of the arena is a great asset. The rider's assignment is to work toward smoothness in being able to execute a circle, then a straight line, a half-turn, a cross-the-diagonal, and so on, in a sequential order.

Classes should work as a large group during the first practice session. Indi-

vidual work should follow to allow the instructor time to correct specific problems. A simple pattern composed of school movements or the ASHA, Training Level Test 1 may be used to determine the riders' proficiency (see Appendix H). If the dressage test is used, place correct dressage letters in the arena; however, it is advisable at this time to allow more working space than that provided by the standard small-size dressage arena. The instructor must be concerned with correctness of bend and smoothness of gait. The size of the arena is of little importance as long as it provides an adequate working area.

Common Problems

1. *Unlevel position of rider's hands when working on a circular track.* Instead of keeping a rein on each side of the horse's neck, the rider allows the inside rein to begin to slip through the hand, thus increasing in length. To compensate for this unnoticed slipping, the rider's hand creeps higher and begins crossing over the withers to the opposite side of the horse's neck. When this happens, the horse does not bend properly in the head and neck but cocks his head. The level of his ears becomes uneven, and his muzzle begins to tip upward (fig. 39).

To correct this situation, the rider must shorten the inside rein, keep the hand down along the side of the horse's neck, squeeze the inside rein slightly, push the horse forward with the legs, and maintain adequate contact on the outside rein to limit the amount of bend desired (fig. 40).

2. *Lack of sufficient pressure applied by the inside leg.* The instructor should hold each student's leg against the horse's side to show the student approximately how much leg pressure is needed. Students must realize that in using the lower leg to generate any movement or

bend the leg does not just lie against the horse. The leg action is press-and-release action, never a steady pressure against the horse's side. Students who ride only in a class and are not physically inclined will be surprised by the amount of muscle needed to bend a horse properly.

BILL CULBERTSON

Fig. 40. When the inside rein is held in the correct position, the horse can be uniformly bent from poll to tail and sufficient forward movement reestablished.

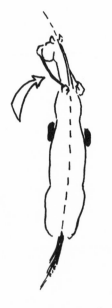

BILL CULBERTSON

Fig. 39. Improper use of the inside rein can result in improper positioning of the head and neck, with insufficient impulsion.

Chapter 5

Body Language Applied

The Halt

In executing a halt, the rider uses the restraining aids. The aids for a halt are, step by step:

1. Check basic position: be sure the torso is elevated, the front line rounded, the shoulder blades together, elbows at the sides, and the weight pushed down through the heel.
2. Brace the back, pushing the spine downward and into the saddle.
3. Position the lower leg behind the girth; close both thighs and lower the legs on the horse.
4. Close both hands simultaneously on the reins and drive the horse into a fixed hand with action of the lower leg.
5. Yield pressure and relax the body as the halt is completed.

With practice these aids are applied simultaneously. As the rider stops the motion of the body, he is saying to the horse, "I'm going to halt; let's halt," and the horse will obey the command if the aids are methodically and consistently applied each time a halt is desired.

In the beginning a horse may not respond immediately to these aids. In asking for a halt, the rider repeats the restraining aids as many times as needed, closing the hands on the reins last, until the horse begins to understand. The rider should always perform a halt in the direction of movement and without loss of balance. The halt is practiced first from a walk and then from a trot and canter. At the trot and canter the halt is performed through the walk. Transitions from a walk to a halt are made until riders have coordinated the use of the aids. When the pace is reduced to a halt, the transition should be smooth and balanced. Such a halt will be possible when riders have control over their backs, legs, and rein aids.

The Half-Halt

A half-halt is a "call to attention." It says to the horse: "We're going to do something different now. Something is going to change." It forewarns the horse that a new direction or action is going to be required. It is a courtesy action to the horse, a "get-ready" signal.

Except for the rein action, the aids for the half-halt are the same as those for a halt, but they are applied to a lesser degree, retarding the horse's action partly instead of fully. In the half-halt it is the degree with which the aids are applied that results in the desired response.

To execute a half-halt:

1. Check basic position: be sure the torso is elevated, the front line rounded, the shoulder blades together, elbows at the sides, and the weight pushed down through the heel.
2. Brace the back, pushing the spine downward and into the saddle.
3. Position the lower leg behind the girth; close both thighs and lower the legs on the horse.
4. Exert soft squeezes on the outside rein. Squeeze and slightly yield without opening the hand or causing slack in the reins.

Transitions

A *transition* is a time of change, or moving from one thing to another. In riding there are two basic transitions: an upward transition and a downward transition.

An upward transition is made when a rider increases the speed or gait of the horse. Walk-trot-canter-gallop is a series of sequential upward transitions. A downward transition is a change in gait characterized by a decrease in speed. Gallop-canter-trot-walk is a series of sequential downward transitions.

To execute a proper upward transition, the rider should half-halt on the outside and then apply the correct aids for a smooth and fluid transition to the desired gait.

To ride a downward transition, a rider executes a series of half-halts until the horse decreases his speed or gait and then relaxes the body (a "go" signal) and sends the horse forward into the desired gait. Horse as well as rider must learn to make smooth transitions. If the horse does not immediately respond to the half-halt, a series of half-halts should follow until he understands what is being asked of him. A correct transition is made smoothly and with as little rein action as possible; therefore, use of the half-halt is essential if a transition is to have a fluid quality.

Students should first practice sequential upward and downward transitions, that is, going from one gait to another without skipping a gait:

Walk—trot—canter (upward)
Canter—trot—walk (downward)

Skip transitions are changes of gait that are not in order of speed progression:

Walk—canter (upward skip transition)
Canter—walk (downward skip transition)
Halt—trot (upward skip transition)
Trot—halt (downward skip transition)

During practice sessions the instructor must be certain that the students understand the aids they are being asked to apply and the effects the aids have on the horses. A thorough understanding of *why* is essential if the rider is to achieve a total communication system with the horse.

Common Problems

1. *Failure of rider to maintain impulsion.*
2. *Improper placement of the horse's head.* In upward transitions the horse is commonly seen traveling with his nose out in front and inclining his head in an

incorrect horizontal position. This head position may also appear during downward transitions owing to lack of impulsion from the hindquarters to push the horse toward the bit. The correction of this problem lies in the use of more leg behind the girth to generate more push from the hind-quarters combined with a steady hand on the reins. The hand must not feed out rein but must instead actively squeeze the heavier rein during a half-halt and subtly use the counter-balance rein to keep the horse's nose in a vertical position. As in all other cases, a rider must use the legs to create impulsion and keep the horse moving toward the bit.

Lateral Bend

Lateral bend refers to the horse's ability to curve or bend his body from head to tail. When a horse is working in the proper shape, he is both laterally bent and vertically flexed. With his whole body rounded the horse pushes forward with the thrust originating from the hindquarters. Before a horse can be put together in the proper shape, he must first be taught to bend his body laterally.

A horse is said to possess the correct degree of lateral bend when his body is bent to the same degree as the circular track on which he is traveling. There-fore, a horse working on a large circle does not require as much bend through-out his body as a horse performing a small circle. The smaller the circle the more lateral bend the horse and rider must achieve (figs. 41A and 41B).

AIDS

Lateral bend is achieved mainly through the use of the rider's inside leg and inside rein. The aids are the same as those

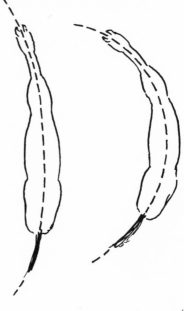

BILL CULBERTSON

Fig. 41A. *The horse possesses the correct degree of lateral bend when his body is bent to the same degree as the circular track on which he is working.*

applied when riding through a turn or corner, but the aids must be maintained throughout the complete circle. The aids for lateral bend are as follows:

1. The inside rein is shortened so that the rider can see the outside corner of the horse's inside eye. The outside hand is moved forward, releasing the same amount of rein as the inside rein is shortened. The outside rein maintains contact with the horse's mouth to control the amount of bend desired.
2. The inside leg is placed at the girth to bend the horse, and the outside leg is placed behind the girth to keep the haunches from falling outside the circle.
3. The inside rein is squeezed like a sponge to keep the horse looking in the

Fig. 41B. Lateral bend to the right. To achieve correct lateral bend, it is imperative that the rider's torso and hand position conform to the arc of the turn or circle being ridden. The rider should look in the direction of travel and position the outside shoulder and hip forward. The inside leg remains at the girth to support the horse's bend, and the outside leg is positioned behind the girth to prevent the quarters from falling out.

direction of travel, while the inside leg, at the girth, and the outside leg, held behind the girth, apply pressure to bend the horse. The inside leg pushes outward in an effort to keep the horse working on the outside rein. Once the inside rein and leg have established a sufficient degree of bend, the rider should lower the knee and heel in the desired direction of travel and push the sitting bone on the corresponding side, slightly forward and to the inside of the circular movement being performed. The inside aids now become passive (inactive), and the turn is actually negotiated with the *outside aids*—the outside rein, leg, and the turning of the rider's torso in the direction of travel. A very active

leg and hand will be necessary at first to maintain the proper degree of bend throughout the movement. Later an active leg and a subtle hand will achieve the same results.

4. The rider's legs, in the correct position, squeeze the horse, sending him forward. Working at a rising trot facilitates the squeezing action. As the rider sits the beat of the rising trot, he should squeeze with the legs.

5. The rider's body must also follow the same curve as the circle on which the horse is traveling. The rider's outside shoulder should be carried slightly forward, while the inside shoulder should be moved back corresponding to the adjustment made in the position of the inside and outside rein.

ARENA EXERCISES

Lateral bend is first practiced at the rising trot because the trot provides more natural impulsion than the walk and is more easily controlled than the canter during introductory work. If the horse begins falling in on his inside shoulder and losing his rhythmic one-two footfall sequence, the rider is placing too much weight on the inside sitting bone, is not using the outside rein sufficiently to control the amount of bend, and is not applying sufficient inside-leg pressure to provide the horse with a support around which to bend.

When riders begin to use the inside leg, tell them to "push the horse to the outside hand." While the horse is bent around the inside leg at the girth, the rider's outside leg completes the bend by holding the hindquarters on the same circle. Action of both legs squeezing in the correct position simultaneously bends the horse, while the inside rein, whose action is limited by the outside rein, correctly positions the horse's head and neck to the proper degree in the direction of travel.

Students will soon understand correct application of the aids, but they will not as readily understand that in riding a circle they do not lean to the inside of the horse but rather place their bodies on the same arc as the circle being ridden. An effective way to demonstrate this action is to outline a circle on the ground with lime and have each student walk around the perimeter, positioning the hands in front as if holding the reins. The student's outside shoulder is slightly forward, and the inside shoulder is slightly back while the student walks the circle, with the body maintaining the same degree of bend as the circle. This exercise should be performed in both directions.

Lateral Bend

Practice sessions for lateral bend begin with simple exercises such as bending the horse through the corner of the arena, riding a half-turn and half-turn in reverse. It will be easier for students to maintain the bend during these movements because they require less muscular control than does riding on a continual circular track.

The instructor asks students to work individually and first perform each figure at a walk. Each student is asked to explain the aids being applied and why they are being used. When each student understands the proper application of the aids, the exercise is repeated in both directions at a rising trot and then at a sitting trot. More advanced exercises to increase lateral bend include the use of serpentines, circles, change of rein through the circle, and the spiral-in.

Serpentine

A serpentine is a continuous series of loops equal in size and shape. A serpentine varies in the number and size of loops depending on the ability of the rider and the size of the arena (figs. 42 and 43).

This exercise is an excellent test of control and use of aids, requiring the rider to look where he is going to maintain loops of uniform size. The first loop is started by moving away from the short side of the arena, and the final loop is finished by moving toward the middle of the opposite short side. The rider never begins or finishes a serpentine by riding into a corner. The rider changes the horse's bend (changes the aids) by using four or five straight steps in the center of each loop. The change is preceded by a half-halt. The horse must be straightened for at least a few steps, or approximately one horse's length, before the new bend is attained. Riding serpentines with

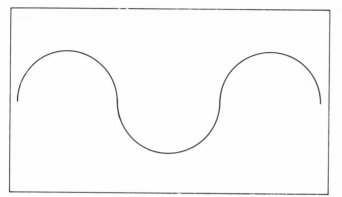

Fig. 42. Exercises using the serpentine require the rider to maintain impulsion while bending and straightening the horse.

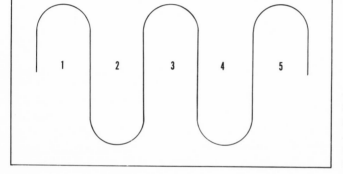

Fig. 43. A serpentine can vary in the number and size of loops according to the rider's ability and the size of the arena.

varying numbers of loops requires the total concentration of the rider and the full attention of the horse.

At first lime can be used to outline the path of the serpentine if students have trouble seeing the path in their minds. Letters can also be used to mark specific points (see figs. 45 and 46).

Circles

Practice riding circles. Use lime to outline a circle if necessary. In the beginning the circles should be no smaller than sixty-six feet in diameter.

Change of Circles

This is a relatively simple circular exercise requiring students to ride a circle, cross the centerline at a right angle,

change the bend, and ride a circle tracking in the opposite direction (fig. 44). Both circles are of uniform size, a half-halt preceding the change of bend that occurs on the straight line before riding the second circle.

Change of Rein Through the Circle

Change of rein through a circle is a means of changing the direction of travel while practicing lateral bend. The rider first rides the perimeter of the circle and at a designated point leaves the perimeter and rides a large S-shaped curve through the center of the circle, thereby changing the rein (fig. 45). When the horse and rider return to the circle, they will be traveling in the opposite direction. As the rider leaves the perimeter of the circle to begin the change of rein, a half-halt

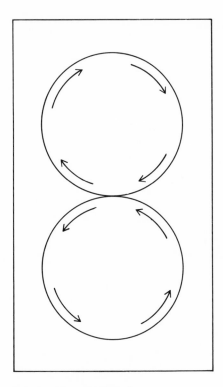

Fig. 44. Change of circles.

diagonal occurs as the change of bend takes place (fig. 46). Both loops of the S, which is actually a serpentine within the circle, should be of uniform size.

Spiral-in

The *spiral-in* is a series of circles, each circle decreasing in size. The rider begins on a very large circle, decreasing the size of each circle while maintaining the bend and rhythm of the stride (fig. 47). As the circle becomes smaller, the exercise increases in difficulty, requiring more active use of the aids and more engagement and impulsion from the horse's hindquarters.

Common Problems

1. *Failure to keep one hand on each side of the horse's neck.*
2. *Application of constant rein pressure, holding instead of squeezing the rein.*
3. *Rider's insufficient use of the inside leg. Rider's lack of muscular strength to do the exercise.*

Putting a Horse Together

Putting a horse together refers to the ability of the rider to place a horse in the proper physical outline to allow him to perform a specific movement. The ele-

is executed to notify the horse of the change in movement, and a half-halt is executed again just before the horse is straightened in the center of the S, and the new bend is assumed. When performed at a rising trot, the change of

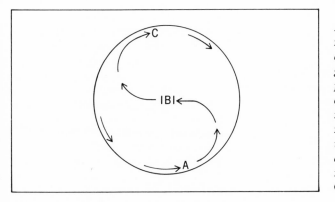

Fig. 45. Change of rein through the circle. The rider begins by trotting the perimeter of the circle on the left rein, leaves the perimeter at A, changes the bend and rising diagonal at B, and returns to the track at C, tracking right.

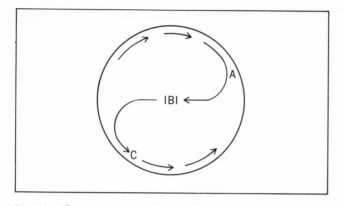

Fig. 46. This exercise is performed beginning on the right rein. The change of rein is made through the circle with the rider continuing on the left rein. Students need to be reminded to maintain sitting-bone influence and proper leg position, lowering the knee and bearing down on the inside heel as they make the change of direction down the centerline.

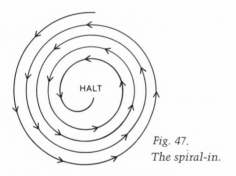

*Fig. 47.
The spiral-in.*

ments associated with the proper shape are lateral bend, vertical flexion, and impulsion. A horse must possess all three of these characteristics to work correctly.

LATERAL BEND—REVIEW

The instructor should review the material above before introducing vertical flexion.

VERTICAL FLEXION

Vertical flexion refers to the position of the horse's head and neck in relation to the ground. The ideal horse's neck should

Fig. 48. The poll is the highest point when the horse exhibits the correct degree of vertical flexion.

be long, allowing the head to be held just in front of the vertical (the vertical being an imaginary straight line drawn perpendicular to the ground). The poll is the highest point when the head and neck are held in correct position. Proper head and neck position allows a rider full use

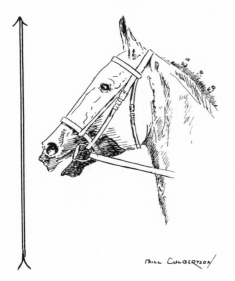

Fig. 49. Above the bit.

Fig. 50. Behind the bit.

of the aids and enables the horse to best utilize his visual properties, while permitting him to best use his head and neck as the balancing apparatus for which they were intended.

Two undesirable head and neck positions that deviate from correct vertical flexion are exhibited in a horse that is "above the bit" and one that is "behind the bit." A horse that is above the bit travels with a raised head, hollow neck and back, and open mouth and gives the general impression of resisting forward movement.

A horse traveling behind the bit is characterized by excessive arching of the neck, the head being tucked inward and down toward the chest. In this instance a point on the crest of the neck rather than the poll is the highest point in the head and neck position, another fault in the horse's general carriage.

IMPULSION

Forward movement in the horse originates from the hindquarters, not from

the forehand. Since the horse's "motor" is in the rear of his "housing," the rider must generate enough thrust (impulsion) to cause the horse to engage the joints of the hind legs, round his back, and push himself forward. Impulsion can be achieved only if the horse is supple and obedient to the rider's aids. The horse must also possess sufficient muscular development to travel with his hindquarters under him. For this reason all prior work has been a methodical progressive schooling program to develop the horse's muscles and make him responsive to aids.

To generate the needed impulsion, the rider must "step on the gas," using the legs behind the girth in a squeezing motion to push the horse forward. A horse is said to be "tracking" when he is traveling with sufficient impulsion, that is, when imprints of the hind feet are placed in or just in front of the prints left by the forefeet (fig. 51).

Sufficient impulsion combined with proper positioning of the head and neck causes the horse to round his back, thereby increasing his ability to carry

Fig. 51. A horse working in the proper shape exhibits a tracking gait. Note the almost uniform distance between the two front feet and the two hind feet. This denotes an even length of stride between the diagonal pair of legs at the trot. The poll is the highest point on the head and neck, and the forehead is slightly in front of the vertical, as verified by the fencepost.

Fig. 52. Rounded surface. This horse looks as though he is moving forward as opposed to the horse in fig. 53. Note the impulsion from the hindquarters, the rounded back, and the nearly vertical head. The horse is steady on the bit, permitting the rider to sit in a relaxed and comfortable manner.

Fig. 53. Hollow surface. This horse exhibits a hollow outline. He lacks impulsion, and his back, head, and neck are not in the proper outline to perform work. To promote impulsion and a rounded back, the rider should lengthen the rein and lower the handle. The horse's head should be vibrated downward, while the rider's leg with the aid of the whip, if necessary, increases the impulsion from behind.

weight (fig. 52). The hollow back that results when a horse is above the bit or lacking in sufficient impulsion does not possess the weight-bearing surface to allow him to carry weight without possible physical discomfort or injury. According to the laws of physics, a rounded surface distributes weight over the surface and downward (toward the rib cage). A hollow surface concentrates all of the weight in the concave area in the hollow of the surface; thus the total mass of weight (the rider) is carried in a very small area (figs. 52 and 53).

TOTAL PHYSICAL OUTLINE,
OR PROPER SHAPE

Traveling on a straight line, a horse is working in the proper shape if he possesses *all* the following characteristics:

1. Sufficient impulsion to cause a tracking gait.
2. Rounded back.
3. Long neck and nearly vertical head.

When working on a circular track, the horse must retain these characteristics while maintaining the necessary degree of lateral bend, determined by the size and shape of the circle or movement being performed.

On the Bit

On the bit refers to the degree of submission or resistance present when a horse is working under saddle. Several elements compose the on-the-bit picture:

1. The horse travels with proper head and neck position.
2. His mouth is closed and relaxed. He

Fig. 54. On the bit. This horse has remained on the bit at the canter depart. Note the levelness of the rider's hands and shoulders. The rider's torso is turned in the direction of travel, while the seat and legs are used to push the horse forward.

does not grind his teeth, loll his tongue, ring his tail, or toss his head.

3. He is responsive to the aids.
4. He exhibits a willingness to move forward.

If a horse is working in the correct physical outline, he will also be working on the bit (fig. 54). The two are inter-related, and all characteristics must be present for the horse to be working properly.

MAINTAINING THE
PROPER SHAPE

A rider working on the rail at a sitting trot uses the following aids to maintain the horse's proper shape:

1. A rider sits on the sitting bones, with the upper body positioned vertically above the hips.

2. The rider drives the horse forward toward the bit by squeezing both legs simultaneously behind the girth.
3. The rider positions one hand on each side of the neck, maintaining light contact with the horse's mouth.
4. The rider's reins are short enough that a soft, squeezing motion on alternate reins helps the horse maintain vertical flexion while the rider's legs continue to drive the horse forward. Once the horse is maintaining the proper head position, only a slight squeezing of the outside rein will be needed to help him maintain vertical flexion.

The position of the rider exerts a marked influence on the horse's ability to perform. The rider should sit back on the sitting bones, open the shoulders, and push the hips slightly forward and in front of the position of the upper body. The rider must remain in balance with the horse and ride in a vertical position to encourage the horse to elevate the forehand.

ARENA EXERCISES

The principles of collection, or shortening the horse's frame, are often difficult for students to grasp and apply. Once they understand the mechanics, begin practice with students working horses first on straight lines—that is, diagonals, center-lines, and cross-the-school—because proper shape is maintained more easily on a straight line than on a circular track.

Begin work at a trot and progress to the canter. While one student works, let another student visually identify whether or not the horse is tracking. Using this visual check method, the instructor is able to determine whether students understand the term *tracking gait.*

When students can work their horses in the proper shape on straight lines, the exercises noted for lateral bend can be used. They will challenge the riders to keep lateral bend, vertical flexion, and impulsion while maintaining the bend on a circular track. These exercises are performed at the trot to take advantage of the natural impulsion provided by this gait.

Several sessions will be required for students to acquire a feel for this kind of riding, and the instructor must prepare lessons containing a variety of interesting exercises to help combat boredom and frustration. The attention span and muscular capabilities of horse and rider may be limited; therefore, frequent short rest periods are recommended.

When resting, encourage the rider to walk the horse quietly on a long frame, allowing him to stretch down toward the ground. Maintain a long contact on the reins by separating the hands and carry-ing them downward toward the knees to encourage the horse to stretch toward

the ground to relax. This will enable the horse to elongate the neck and back muscles that are being used when the horse is working in the proper shape (figs. 55A and 55B).

Common Problems

1. *The rider fails to send the horse forward with sufficient impulsion for the horse to maintain his shape and stay on the bit.* Work without stirrups will help riders emphasize the use of the lower leg. Maintaining a light contact with the horse's mouth is essential, and the reins must be held short enough to allow a gentle squeeze on either rein to correct faulty head and neck position as the legs continue to drive the horse forward. The use of the reins to maintain vertical flexion without the reinforcement of leg aids results in an artificial head set. There is no rounding of the horse's back, and the horse lacks sufficient impulsion from the hindquarters (fig. 56). A rider must learn continually to send the horse forward with the legs while using the hand to position the head and neck.

2. *The rider mistakes impulsion for propulsion and lets the horse race for-ward, exerting no limitation of pace through the use of the reins.* As the rider's legs generate the push, the hands and reins must work with the legs to limit the degree to which the horse can move forward. In this way the horse must engage the joints of the hind legs, bring his hind legs up under his body, and push forward while a steady hand acts as a gentle barrier saying, "No, you can't race forward." The forward push and gentle limitation cause the horse's energy to travel from the hindquarters, through the back, neck, and head, rounding the whole body.

3. *The rider has the tendency to pitch forward on the crotch instead of sitting back on the sitting bones.* The caution "Upper body back" will help correct this

Fig. 55A and B. To relax the horse after a work session, continue to use him to walk energetically forward, and gradually lengthen the reins to allow him to extend and lower the head and neck, thus stretching the muscles in the neck and back.

Fig. 56. Use of the reins to maintain vertical flexion without the reinforcement of the leg aids can result in an artificial head set, no rounding of the back, and insufficient impulsion from the hindquarters.

position if the student tends to ride in front of the vertical.

4. *The rider rounds the shoulders and slouches forward.* To correct this problem, ask the rider to take a shallow breath and carry a small amount of air in the lungs to elevate the rib cage and then rotate the shoulders backward and stretch the torso upward.

The Sitting Trot

Introduce the sitting trot after students are fairly well balanced at the three basic gaits and are able to maintain a steady hand position while riding through school movements. Riders will soon discover that sitting the trot requires much more skill and muscle control than rising

at the trot. The rider must sit in a vertical position, keep the spine straight and push it forward and well into the saddle, and close the lower leg on the horse to drive it forward. The hands remain steady and light. As the rider drives the horse forward onto the bit, the bit acts as a balancing apparatus, or "fifth leg," allowing the horse to steady himself and maintain a rhythmic gait.

LESSON PROCEDURE

The sitting trot is developed from the rising trot and is introduced in the following procedure:

Students are asked to perform a rising trot on the rail. Once the trot is established, ask the students to reduce the height of the rising motion gradually until each is posting without leaving the seat of the saddle. The forward-and-back motion of the post is then maintained through hip motion while the rider's seat remains in the saddle.

While the "posting-without-leaving-the-saddle" action may at first appear exaggerated, the rider will soon realize that to sit the trot one must push the back forward and swing with every trot stride. The horse's stride can be lengthened or shortened depending on the rider's ability to sit securely into the saddle and lengthen or lighten and shorten the swing. When added impulsion is required, the rider's legs are squeezed well behind the girth. The hand maintains the selected frame and prevents the horse from breaking gait.

As students become proficient in working a horse in the proper shape, the sitting trot will be more easily performed. The roundness of the horse's frame is the essential element permitting a rider to learn to sit at both the trot and the canter.

ARENA EXERCISES

Use the rising trot during a warm-up period to allow the rider to move rhythmically with the horse's stride and remove weight from the horse's back, thus enabling him to stretch his back muscles before the rider begins to sit continually in the saddle.

The objectives of a warm-up session at the rising trot should be to

1. Determine the energy level of the horse.
2. Lengthen the muscles of both horse and rider so that they are ready to perform work.
3. Encourage the student to move the horse sufficiently forward so that the

sitting trot can be developed; if the horse lacks forward movement, it is difficult to perform either a rising trot or a sitting trot.

While practicing the sitting trot, the rider must be careful to maintain the correct position. As fatigue occurs, allow the rider to post at will or rest briefly at a walk.

The basic balanced-seat position, which requires a vertical seat, must be maintained. Have the students carry the arms close to the sides with a bend in each elbow. If straightening of the arms begins to occur, ask the riders to "carry an elbow on each side seam." The elbows are never permitted to slip backward from this point. The hands must remain low and steady. The rider's left hand is carried on the left side of the horse, and the right hand is carried on the right side of the horse. At no time should either hand cross the horse's withers. The lower leg remains under the rider's body to be used behind the girth to send the horse forward. The upper body exhibits a rounded front line, and the head is held squarely over the shoulders on a horizontal plane.

When sufficient forward motion can be maintained, have the rider practice the sitting trot on the rail. As the rider's proficiency develops, school movements utilizing straight lines can be ridden. When harmony between horse and rider is evident and the horse's gait remains rhythmic and undisturbed, large school movements utilizing a circular track may also be employed.

Common Problems

1. *Insufficient independence between the rider's seat and hands.* The solution to this problem lies in continual practice in keeping the hands steady and low, one on each side of the horse's withers. Exercises on the longe will also help a student develop an independent seat.

2. *Lack of sufficient muscle power and coordination to sit the trot.* This problem and that of developing an independent seat and hands are interrelated, and as improvement in one area is achieved, the other problem will also begin to rectify itself.

3. *The tendency for a rider to slouch and rotate the shoulders forward.* This position pulls the rider's seat from the saddle, which makes it impossible to sit the trot. The correction is to lengthen the reins so that the rider can sit comfortably in a vertical position with a bend in the elbows. The bend in the elbows allows the rider to carry the hands low without removing the seat from the saddle. This position also allows the rider to continue to push the horse forward with seat and legs as the sitting trot is maintained. The rider must now be asked to rotate the shoulders backward and round the front line. This position allows the rider's back to remain straight, while the rounded front line serves to push the spine downward into the seat, which in turn increases the rider's ability to sit.

4. *Failure to maintain rein contact.* Driving the horse toward the bit without pulling back on the reins or losing contact is difficult to overcome. Independence of hand and seat will help alleviate the problem. The hands must be held in a steady position, while a soft alternate squeezing of the hand promotes a soft contact with the horse's mouth and helps discourage the horse from leaning on the bit. The rider must concentrate on sending the horse forward from the hindquarters through the use of legs and seat rather than trying to encourage forward movement by slackening the reins.

Rhythm

As students begin truly working their horses, requiring them to bend, maintain the proper shape, and respond to active aids, they will also become conscious of the rhythm of each gait. Rhythm is the regularity of footfalls within each gait. The walk, having a footfall pattern 1-2-3-4, has the same time interval between each step. The walk consists of four regularly timed or spaced beats. It must not consist of short and long strides. Each stride should cover the same amount of ground with clocklike precision. The two-beat trot and the three-beat canter should also consist of regular, consistent strides, all the strides the same length.

Each horse has a particular rhythm and length of stride in which he is most comfortable. Some horses lack a consistent rhythm, while others lose their rhythm on corners or when asked to execute small movements such as a *volte* (a six-meter circle).

ARENA EXERCISES

It is the rider's responsibility to help the horse maintain a steady rhythm throughout each gait. To instill in students the rhythm of each gait, ask them to count the number of beats in each gait as each foot hits the ground. Verbalizing the rhythm helps students determine whether or not the gait is steady.

Another exercise is to have each student hold the reins in the outside hand and place the inside hand on the seat of the saddle. The rider then sits on the hand. Through the hand the rider's own movement can be felt, allowing the rider to determine whether or not the footfall sequence for each gait occurs at regularly spaced intervals. During this exercise students count the beats of each gait so that the footfall sequence will become established in their minds.

Emphasize the importance of the rhythmic quality of the horse's gait, explaining that smoothness of gait and evenness of stride are performance characteristics required in the show ring and in dressage. Rhythmic gaits result in a smoother ride and enhance the over-all appearance and performance of the working horse.

Lengthening the Stride

"A horse should be like a rubber band that can lengthen and shorten without resistance," Colonel Bengt Ljungquist, past coach of the United States Dressage Team, has said.

The rubber-band principle refers to the horse's ability to shorten and lengthen his frame and stride without loss of balance or rhythm while exhibiting marked obedience to the aids.

The mechanics of lengthening the stride have a "round-robin" effect in that adequate engagement of the hind legs allows a prolonged moment of suspension, which in turn allows the forelegs to stretch forward, giving the hind legs time to bend and engage sufficiently, which again prolongs the moment of suspension. Then the cycle begins again. It is essential that students understand the mechanics, or the result will be not a true lengthening but simply an increased number of short, choppy steps.

AIDS TO LENGTHENING
THE STRIDE

To lengthen the stride, the rider maintains a vertical seat, gives slightly through the reins to allow the horse to lengthen head and neck, and increases impulsion by closing the legs well behind the girth and increasing the length of the forward swing created by the rider's upper body. To shorten the stride, the rider executes a half-halt, slightly shortens the reins to shorten the frame, lightens the driving action of the seat, and maintains sufficient leg pressure to ensure adequate impulsion.

The horse may seek additional contact with the bit during the lengthening process, and the rider must be careful that the horse does not begin to lean. Should the horse begin to lean, the rider should squeeze one rein and yield, then squeeze the other rein and yield. At the same time the rider must be careful to continue to squeeze with the legs to maintain impulsion from the hindquarters.

ARENA EXERCISES

1. The horse is ridden in a collected frame along the short side of the arena and through the corner. A half-halt is then executed, and the stride lengthened down the long wall. Before reaching the next corner, the horse is returned to a collected frame (figs. 57A and 57B). If the horse resists the return to a collected frame, have the student ride him on a circle to collect him before continuing the exercise. This exercise should be mastered at the trot and then executed at the canter.

2. The horse is collected along the short side and ridden through the corner. A half-halt calls the horse to attention, and he is then ridden across the diagonal at a lengthened stride. The horse's frame should be shortened before the diagonal is completed so that a smooth change of rein can be made (figs. 58A and 58B). This exercise can also be performed on the centerline. Lengthening across the diagonal should be performed only at a trot.

Common Problems

1. *The horse's head is held too high, and the neck remains too short.* To solve this problem, the rider lengthens the reins, lowers both hands toward the thighs, and exert a squeezing action with each rein (one rein and then the other).

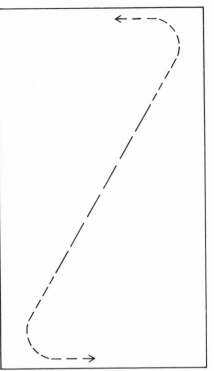

*Fig. 57A. The horse must be allowed
to lengthen his frame to be able to
lengthen his stride.*

*Fig. 57B. Shortening and lengthening
the stride make an excellent gymnastic
exercise for the horse and require the
rider to use the half-halt effectively
and coordinate hand and leg aids.*

2. *The horse's steps are short and
choppy rather than long and smooth.*
The rider must increase the use of the leg
aids to achieve more impulsion. Check to
be sure that the rider is not holding the
reins too tight. See also the correction for
problem 1 above.

3. *The horse's movement becomes
tense and jerky.* The rider should try to
relax and push the horse forward on a
long frame.

4. *Change of rhythm between collected
and lengthened work.* The rider must
maintain impulsion throughout all exercises. Emphasize use of the half-halt

while maintaining impulsion during
transitions.

5. *The horse begins to lean on the bit.*
The rider should squeeze one rein and
then the other to remove a constant bit
surface on which the horse can lean.

6. *The rider's hands are not held low
and steady.* The rider should regularly
check on the position of the hands and
consciously work to keep them low and
steady to enable the horse to work in the
proper shape.

7. *Insufficient use of the driving aids.*
The rider must use leg aids more actively
behind the girth to push the horse forward.

Fig. 58A. *Lengthened stride at the trot, rising. As the rider asks the horse to lengthen his frame and go forward, the hands become more separated and remain low to free the horse's shoulders and allow him to lengthen his stride. The poll remains the highest point, and the horse's head is carried slightly in front of the vertical.*

Fig. 58B. *Lengthened stride at the canter. The rider has released the horse from the hand and pushes with the seat and legs to send the horse forward in a lengthened frame. Light contact remains with the horse's mouth; the separated hands free the shoulder to allow increased movement. The horse should not become heavy in the forehand. The poll remains the highest point, and the head is carried slightly in front of the vertical.*

Simple Change of Lead

Students should now be able to ride a circle at a working canter, maintaining a fair degree of lateral bend, vertical flexion, and impulsion. When the proper shape has been established, work on simple lead changes can begin.

A simple change of lead is performed when a horse working at a canter drops to a trot, changes his direction of travel, and resumes the canter on the opposite lead. For example, a horse cantering on the left rein drops to a trot, changes direction, and resumes the canter on the right rein, thus traveling on the right lead.

Executing a simple change of lead will not be difficult for students, providing they can apply the aids correctly and understand the necessity of having the horse correctly bent in the direction of travel. Several exercises provide an excellent means for teaching the simple change. They are the half-turn, the change of rein through the circle, the change of circles (figure-eight) and the serpentines. While almost all school movements allow the rider to perform a simple change, the exercises listed above provide the rider with extra help, since a circular figure encourages the rider to apply the aids correctly and positions the horse to pick up the desired lead properly. While learning to put a horse in the proper shape is more easily accomplished on a straight line, basic work in simple changes is more easily performed by using a circular track.

STEPS IN A SIMPLE CHANGE OF LEAD

The following steps should be followed to execute a simple change of lead:

1. Ride the circular figure with the proper degree of bend—half-halt.
2. Drop to a trot at the designated point, straighten the horse for five or six steps, or approximately one horse's length—half-halt.
3. Assume the new bend.
4. Apply the aids for the canter and lead desired.

ARENA EXERCISES

Use the exercises shown in figures 59 to 62 during basic practice sessions.

Each figure indicates the direction of travel and the points at which the horse drops to a trot, straightens, assumes the new bend, and travels in the opposite direction. Have the students perform all the exercises in both directions of travel. The figure eight is considered a change of circles. Ideally all circular figures and loops should be of uniform size.

ADVANCED EXERCISES

Once the riders are capable of performing a simple change utilizing the bend in the figure as an aid, have them perform all simple changes on a straight line. At this point use the following exercises shown in figures 63 and 64.

An example of a simple pattern that can be used in advanced work is shown in figure 65.

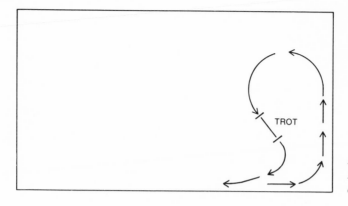

Fig. 59.
Half-turn, simple
change of lead.

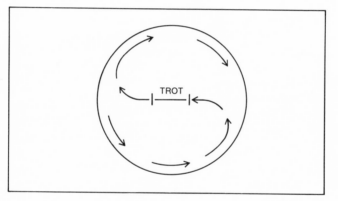

Fig. 60.
Change of rein
through the circle,
simple change
of lead.

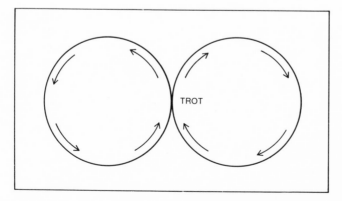

Fig. 61.
Change of circles,
simple change
of lead.

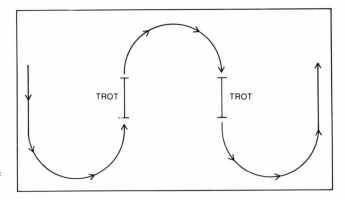

Fig. 62.
Serpentine, simple
change of lead.

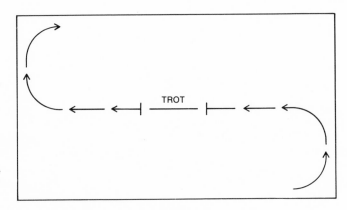

Fig. 63.
Up the centerline,
simple change
of lead.

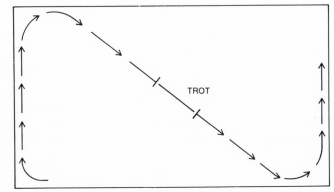

Fig. 64.
Cross-the-diagonal,
simple change
of lead.

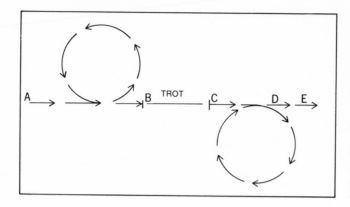

Fig. 65.
Pattern utilizing
the simple change
of lead.
A: *Begin at trot,
pick up left lead,
circle left.*
B–C: *Trot, straighten
horse, pick up right
lead, circle.*
D: *Trot.* E: *Halt.*

As the instructor notes a measure of proficiency in the performing of simple changes, the number of trot steps should be reduced until the student is able to execute a simple change with only two trot steps and then one trot step. When that is accomplished, the horse will be working off the rear quarters, and the rider will be coordinating all aids effectively.

Common Problems

1. *The rider leans to the inside to execute a simple change.* The rider must be encouraged to use all the aids for a canter when asking for a simple change of lead. This means that the rider must reverse the lower-leg position, change the sitting-bone influence, and readjust the position of the reins. When a rider leans to one side, the horse has a natural tendency to move under the rider's weight. This means that when a rider leans to the inside the horse adjusts a major portion of his weight to his inside shoulder. While sitting-bone influence remains slightly dominant in the direction of travel, the rider must remain centered on the horse, turning the body without leaning in the direction the horse is to go.

2. *The rider fails to maintain contact on the reins.* When this occurs, the horse is permitted to run forward and fall on his forehand instead of placing his hind legs under his body and picking himself up to assume the canter in the new direction. Taking time to half-halt, methodically drop to a trot, maintain rein contact, half-halt again, and correctly apply the aids will help correct this problem. Riders should not be allowed to incline the upper body forward or let the elbows straighten during the simple change of lead; either error will cause a loss of rein contact.

3. *Reappearance of old problems.* Old problems may reappear as new material is presented. Review and reinforce correct methods along with practice sessions.

Leg Yield

The leg yield is a suppling exercise. It makes a horse responsive to unilateral aids (hand and leg on the same side) and the dominant diagonal aids in this exercise, the inside leg and outside rein. It also prepares a horse for advanced work, such as shoulder-in, half-pass, haunches-

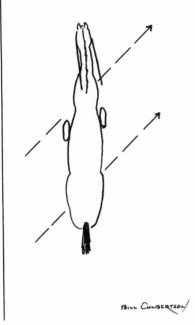

BILL CULBERTSON

Fig. 66. During the leg-yielding exercise the horse is bent slightly away from the direction of travel as he moves obliquely forward.

in, and haunches-out. It requires the rider to coordinate the use of various aids to maintain rhythm and proper movement of the horse.

The instructor should teach leg yielding before the turn on the forehand, for it is easier for students to influence a horse that is in motion. Leg yielding, which can be executed without a great deal of collection, makes an excellent exercise to give students the feel of moving forward and sideways simultaneously. Use this exercise first at a walk and then at a trot; it is easier to maintain a horse's forward movement and create impulsion at this gait. Leg yielding is executed with the horse looking *away* from the direction of

travel. Because leg yielding will be converted into the half-pass—a lateral movement in which the horse moves obliquely forward as in leg yielding but looks *in* the direction of travel—it is important not to overbend the horse away from the direction of travel when practicing leg-yielding exercises (fig. 66). Sufficient bend is obtained when the rider can see the eyebrow and nostril on the inside of the horse. A leg-yielding exercise can be ridden across the diagonal, away from a long wall, away from a long wall and back to the long wall, and on a circle.

STEPS IN LEG YIELDING

1. Half-halt.
2. Bend the horse slightly away from the direction of travel. Maintain weight to the inside of the horse.
3. Use the inside leg behind the girth to push the horse sideways.
4. Use the outside leg at the girth to maintain impulsion and to help keep the horse straight while preventing overbending.
5. With the inside rein maintain the bend.
6. With the outside rein limit the bend and lead the horse sideways and forward in the desired direction.
7. Look in the direction of movement and at the point of destination.

ARENA EXERCISES

1. Leg yielding away from a long wall is one of the simplest ways to acquaint students with this exercise. The horse and rider begin leg yielding away from a long wall to the center of the arena. At the center the horse is straightened and ridden forward (fig. 67). If the rider fails to maintain sufficient impulsion and forward movement at any time

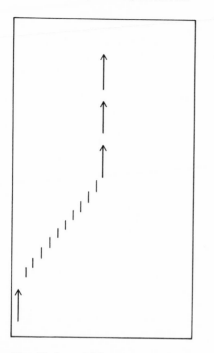

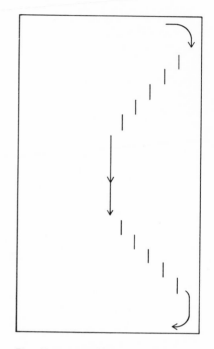

Fig. 67. Leg yielding away from a long wall.

Fig. 68. Leg yielding away from and back to a long wall.

during the exercise, have him straighten the horse, reestablish the rhythm, and continue the exercise.

2. In leg yielding across the diagonal, the rider passes through the corner, bends the horse away from the direction of travel, and pushes him sideways across the diagonal. Coordinating the aids previously noted, the rider always looks at the point of destination. For example, a rider working on the right rein rides through the corner, half-halts, bends the horse slightly to the left, places the inside (left) leg behind the girth to push the horse sideways, places the right (outside) leg on the girth to help maintain impulsion, and uses the left rein to maintain the bend and the right rein to lead the horse across the diagonal. Throughout the movement the rider looks across the diagonal at the point of destination.

Have the students practice this exercise in both directions (fig. 68).

3. The horse is moved away from a long wall to the center of the arena and straightened for one horse length, the bend is changed to the opposite direction, and leg yielding is performed back to the long wall (fig. 69).

4. Leg yielding on a circle helps correct a horse that tries to cut corners or execute a smaller circle than the one desired. The same aids are applied, the only difference being that the horse is now traveling on a circular track rather than on a straight line. The rider pushes the horse out on the circle, using the inside leg behind the girth while maintaining the bend and forward motion of the horse (fig. 70).

Leg yielding can be used in show-ring riding when a horse needs to be moved out toward the rail without sacrificing

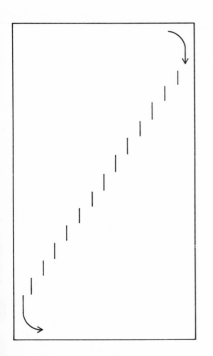

Fig. 69. Leg yielding across the diagonal.

the required bend. For example, a horse traveling on the left rein in an English Pleasure class may try to cut a corner. The rider should push the horse back out to the rail by applying pressure with the left leg slightly behind the girth and subtly lead the horse out with the right rein while maintaining the required bend to the left. Responding to these aids, the horse should move out toward

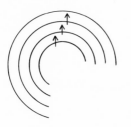

Fig. 70. Leg yielding on a circle.

the rail and continue on in the proper shape. Leg yielding can be performed at any of the three gaits.

Common Problems

1. *Lack of forward movement resulting in too much crossing over.* This problem is caused by insufficient use of the rider's legs to maintain impulsion. The rider should use the inside leg slightly behind the girth to push the horse sideways and at the same time use an active outside leg at the girth to maintain sufficient forward motion. The rider should also check to be sure that the reins are not being held too tight, because that will also impede forward motion.

2. *Haunches lead.* This faulty position is due to too much bend in the horse's head and neck. To correct the problem, the rider should lengthen the inside rein and shorten the outside rein to decrease the bend in the horse's head and neck and also decrease the use of the inside leg to push the horse sideways and increase the use of the outside leg positioned at the girth to maintain impulsion and help keep the horse's body straight.

3. *Horse overbent.* This problem may result from too short an inside rein and insufficient contact on the outside rein to limit (stop) the bend. Contact on the outside rein should be increased along with more substantial use of the outside leg at the girth to help straighten the horse and maintain impulsion.

4. *Lack of rhythm.* This problem may be caused by overbending, too much crossing over, not enough forward motion, or insufficient use of the lower leg. If the horse is overbent, the rider should increase forward motion, check for unnecessary rein pressure, and increase the use of the outside leg.

5. *Rider collapses a hip.* A rider may collapse a hip in an effort to increase the strength in the leg required to exert pressure to displace the horse sideways.

In collapsing a hip, the rider leans to the side on which the leg is being used. This incorrect position of the rider's upper body adversely influences a horse's balance, ability to carry weight, and ability to perform a movement correctly. Have the rider raise the shoulder, inhale, and maintain a small amount of air in his lungs to elevate the rib cage and maintain an erect upper-body position.

Turn on the Forehand

The turn on the forehand is an introduction to movement that does not consist of forward motion. It teaches the rider to use several aids simultaneously, supples the horse, makes him obedient to the aids, and causes him to move away from leg pressure, a response that is necessary for any movement to be accomplished correctly. Care must be taken not to override this turn, since it may cause resistance when the horse is asked to perform the proper turn, the turn on the haunches.

STEPS IN A TURN ON THE FOREHAND

The turn on the forehand is practiced in three stages: beside a long wall (or fence) in the arena, off the wall, and off the wall with the horse maintaining the proper degree of vertical flexion.

Beside a Long Wall

The rider rides parallel to a wall or fence and halts squarely. The rider drops the stirrups and crosses them over the horse's neck to allow the lower leg more freedom of movement. The reins are held short enough to control the position of the horse's head and neck and prevent him from moving forward. During the initial stage of training, the horse's head is positioned slightly to the inside so that the rider can see the outside corner of the inside eye. The rider's inside leg is placed well behind the girth to push the hindquarters toward the center of the arena. The rider's outside leg is slightly behind the girth to stop the horse's sideways motion. The rider pushes with the

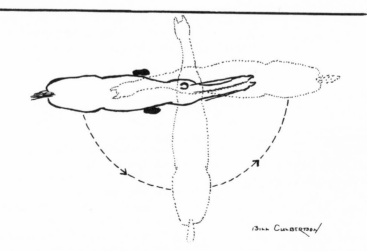

Fig. 71. Turn on the forehand beside a long wall.

inside leg, the horse takes a step, and the rider catches (stops) the horse's movement with the outside leg (fig. 71). Remind the riders that the term *inside* always refers to the direction of the horse's bend.

If the horse performs a turn on the forehand correctly, the inside forefoot will be picked up and returned to the same place. It should not pivot and remain "screwed" into the ground without being lifted and replaced. The outside forefoot steps forward and around the inside forefoot, while the hind feet move on a curved line, the inside hind foot striking the ground in front of the outside hind foot.

Off the Wall

When a quarter-turn on the forehand can be executed step by step parallel to the wall, have the rider practice the movement away from the wall.

ADDITION OF VERTICAL FLEXION

A turn on the forehand in its finished stages is performed with a horse standing squarely and exhibiting vertical flexion without visible turning of the head when the movement is executed. A finished turn on the forehand may be either 90 or 180 degrees, that is, a quarter or half-turn in either direction.

Common Problems

1. *The horse moves forward.* To correct this problem, halt the horse and begin again. Insufficient contact on the reins or reins that are too long can cause this problem.

2. *The horse moves backward.* The rider should immediately push the horse forward several steps to communicate to the horse that backward movement is incorrect. It is not enough to move the

horse forward one or two steps; that is not sufficient movement to communicate clearly to the horse his mistake. The rider should move the horse ahead five or six steps, enough to say, "No, your reaction was wrong." Cause for this evasion may be too tight a restraining rein or an unconscious backward pressure on the reins.

3. *The horse moves sideways.* When this evasion occurs, the rider should use the leg slightly behind the girth on the side of the horse to which it is moving. This pushes the horse over and straightens his body. It may be necessary for the rider to tap the horse on the shoulder if he tries to move his forehand to the side.

For example, if a horse moves sideways to the left, the rider's left leg should apply pressure slightly behind the girth to move the horse's body to the right. If the horse moves his forehand to the left, the rider should tap the horse's left shoulder with a whip to correct the action. If the horse has been taught to move away from applied pressure, the problem can be corrected.

4. *The horse's head and neck are overbent.* If the rider can see more than the outside corner of the inside eye, the horse is overbent for a turn on the forehand. Contact on the outside rein should be increased, and the inside rein should be lengthened proportionally to help rectify the problem.

5. *The reins are overused; insufficient use of the rider's legs.* The role of the hands on the reins is to position the horse's head and neck; the rider's legs must accomplish the turn through methodically applied directional pressure.

6. *The rider twists the upper body.* This may occur when the rider is trying to give the inside leg added strength. Have the rider return the upper body to the correct erect position and use the legs to accomplish the turn.

Introduction to a Dressage Test

Dressage is a time-tested, methodical progression of exercises designed to increase a horse's muscular capabilities and degree of suppleness, allowing him to perform increasingly difficult movements under saddle. Within the dressage system are various levels of tests designed to examine a horse's ability to perform specific movements. These levels range from the training level, which consists of movements in simple straight lines and large circles, to the *grand prix* level, which calls for half-pass, piaffe, passage, flying change of lead, pirouette, and collected and extended gait. As a horse's training progresses, the tests become more difficult, testing not only the horse's ability to perform but also the rider's ability to be a harmonious partner with his horse.

Student proficiency at the intermediate level of equitation can be tested with the ASHA Training Level Tests 1 and 2. All the movements required in these tests have been presented in class material. For complete information concerning dressage competition, students should refer to a current AHSA rulebook.

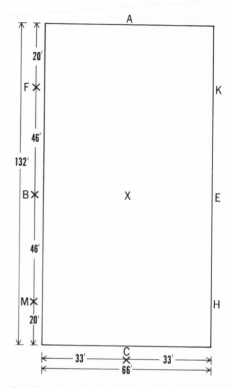

Fig. 72. Dimensions of a small dressage arena.

THE DRESSAGE ARENA

Level ground with good footing is essential for a dressage arena. The lower-level tests may be ridden in a small arena measuring 20 by 40 meters (66 by 132 feet). Third-level tests and above must be ridden in the standard arena, which measures 20 by 60 meters (66 by 198 feet). Specific letters that never change position mark points along the perimeter of the arena (fig. 72). These letters designate the exact spot where a movement begins or ends.

Whenever possible, construct the arena on a north-south plane to prevent sun interference. An X denotes the center of the arena, but it is not visibly marked (fig. 73). The rider always enters at A. When there is only one judge, the judge and jury (the judge and a writer) are always seated outside the arena at C. The arena fence should be approximately twelve inches high. It can be made of light sections of round poles painted white. If a permanent structure is not available, mark the corners of the arena with white ground poles; the letters serve as the other reference points.

RIDING A TEST

First, establish an order of "go." As one rider finishes the test, have the next rider ready and waiting to enter at A. It is advisable for the incoming rider to keep

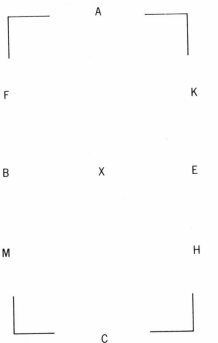

Fig. 73. *A small dressage arena set up with corner poles and letters.*

up at the judge, and smiles (saluting with the interior of the hat facing the judge makes a rider appear to be seeking a donation). He then returns the hat to the head and secures it in place with the hand remaining on the brim. It is incorrect for the rider to replace the hat and then use the hand to secure it by pushing down the crown. The judge acknowledges the salute with a nod of the head, signaling the rider to proceed. The rider returns the reins to two hands, executes a smooth transition to trot, and begins the test.

Each movement begins or ends with the rider's shoulder parallel with the designated letter. An early or late transition may be partly excused at the training level if the transition is smooth and fluid, but the rider must strive for the precision required in higher-level tests.

During the test riders should remember to breathe regularly to help relieve tension. Many riders tend to hold their breath when concentrating, and this exerts a negative effect on the body, making it tense. The tension is communicated to the horse, and the result is often a jerky performance. After the final halt and salute the ride is not over until horse and rider have left the arena at a free walk on a loose rein. For this reason the rider should wait until the complete exit has been made before rewarding the horse for his performance or making any verbal comments.

the horse moving while waiting to begin, to help prevent a sluggish entrance. When the judge signals for the next rider by ringing a bell, the incoming rider has one minute in which to enter the arena. When the bell is rung, the entering rider should trot a circle or two outside the A marker to establish the horse's tempo and then proceed into the arena straight down the centerline at a sitting trot, halt and salute at X. During the halt the horse should stand squarely and remain immobile and on the bit. To salute, the rider holds both reins in the left hand. A woman drops the right hand behind the right thigh, bows the head for a moment, and then looks up at the judge and smiles. A man removes his hat with the right hand, drops the right hand behind the right thigh with the crown of the hat facing the judge, looks

RULES

The following rules should be observed during a ride:

1. Riding with both hands is obligatory.
2. If a rider goes off course, the judge rings a bell and informs the rider at which letter to resume the test.
3. If the test is read, each movement may

be called only once. The reader stands outside the arena beside either E or B and reads one movement ahead of the movement being performed.

4. No clucking or vocal commands are permitted.

5. Elimination results from the following: the horse leaving the arena with all four feet, leaving the arena at the end of a ride in any way other than at the letter A, the horse entering with the tongue tied down, failure to enter the ring within one minute of the bell, or the accumulation of three errors. When elimination occurs, the horse and rider are permitted to complete the test.

SCORING

Each movement is scored on a scale from 0 to 10 according to the horse's performance.

10—Excellent	3—Fairly Bad
9—Very Good	2—Bad
8—Good	1—Very Bad
7—Fairly Good	0—Not performed or
6—Satisfactory	fall of horse and
5—Sufficient	rider
4—Insufficient	

Penalties (errors):

First error—2 points off
Second error—4 points off
Third error—elimination

TACK

Lower-level tests, up to or including third or fourth levels, are ridden in a plain snaffle with or without a dropped noseband. Beginning at third level, a double bridle may be used at the rider's discretion. Saddles may be forward-seat, all-purpose, or dressage style.

ATTIRE

Proper dress should not be mandatory in a class; however, students must know the acceptable attire for the show arena.

Proper attire varies according to the size and stature of the show, but it is always conservative, with neatness being of prime importance. For schooling shows a hacking jacket, shirt and stock tie, hunt cap, breeches, and boots are suitable. For a larger show appropriate attire at lower levels is buff-, canary- or stone-colored breeches, white shirt, stock tie and plain gold safety pin, black boots, black coat, black hunt cap, and black gloves. Spurs are optional at lower levels.

Full dress is optional beginning with the third level and becomes mandatory above the fourth level. Full dress is generally associated with the use of a double bridle. Full dress includes a top hat, cutaway coat with tails, white shirt, stock tie with gold safety pin, white breeches, black boots, spurs, and white gloves.

Jewelry is discouraged because it detracts from the desired tailored appearance of the rider. One whip may be carried into the arena in training through level 4 except in AHSA qualifying and championship classes (see Appendix H for AHSA Training Level Tests 1 and 2).

BRAIDING

Horses shown in dressage should have the mane and forelock braided with yarn or taped with one-half-inch white adhesive tape. The braid may be the traditional dressage braid or an acceptable variation. The tail is left unbraided, natural and flowing.

Chapter 6

Introduction to Forward-Seat Riding

The key to successful riding is a flexible seat—the ability to adapt the seat for the terrain being covered or movement being performed. Up to this point students have used the balanced or dressage seat for work on the flat. In this vertical seat weight is distributed over a three-point contact—the rider's seat and both legs. The leg is long to allow maximum contact with the horse and maximum use of the leg aids. The seat allows the rider to collect the horse and requires the horse's hindquarters to act as the weight-bearing surface, allowing the forehand to remain light and elevated. When a horse is to work in a collected frame and exhibit the characteristics of an elevated forehand and lowered and pushing hindquarters, he must adjust his center of gravity slightly to the rear. To remain in equilibrium with the horse, the rider must sit erect in a full seat with the weight distributed on both sitting bones.

Balance, the common equilibrium of the horse and rider, is an essential ingredient for any harmonious action. The horse's center of gravity, or balance, is adjusted slightly to the rear to achieve collection and is adjusted forward during extended movements. In work over uneven terrain and jumping, the horse's center of gravity is shifted forward. To remain in common equilibrium with the horse, the rider must adjust the position forward and use the forward seat to remove weight from the horse's back, unburden the hindquarters, and maintain common equilibrium.

Chart 1 compares the physical outline of the horse when he is working in balanced seat and forward seat and when jumping.

CHART 1. *Physical Outline of the Horse*

Balanced Seat (Dressage)	Forward Seat	Jumping
Rounded back	Rounded back	Rounded back
Impulsion from hindquarters	Impulsion from hindquarters	Impulsion from hindquarters
Vertical head	Less-vertical head	Freedom to stretch head and neck for balance
Center of gravity slightly toward rear	Center of gravity slightly toward forehand	Center of gravity toward forehand
Hindquarters serve as weight-bearing surface for collected movements	Hindquarters push and propel horse forward	Hindquarters push and propel horse forward
Elevated forehand	Less elevation of forehand on the flat	Less elevation of forehand on the flat
Usually a collected frame on the flat	A more lengthened frame on flat	Lengthened or shortened frame as needed

Chart 2 compares the basic positions of the rider when working in balanced seat and forward seat and when jumping.

Forward-Seat Position

Forward seat is the style of riding that permits the rider to sit closer to the forehand and permits adjustment of the center of gravity forward to negotiate obstacles and remove the weight (seat) from the saddle when necessary.

There are two basic positions in forward-seat riding. One position is taken when hacking (riding) on the flat. The rider utilizes the three points of contact in the seat—the crotch and the two sitting bones as in the balanced seat (figs. 74A and 74B). The other is the jump position, also called the half-seat and the two-point contact. This position is taken when riding over uneven terrain or negotiating obstacles. To attain the position, the rider drops all the weight into the thighs, knees, and heels, removing the seat from the saddle (fig. 75).

When utilizing the forward seat, the rider shortens the stirrup leathers approximately two holes so that the tread of the irons hangs at the anklebone. As the foot is inserted in the stirrup, the rider finds that the leg is considerably shorter. While additional bend in the knee and a shorter base of support from the lower leg make it possible for the rider to get up out of

CHART 2. *Rider Position*

Balanced Seat (Dressage)	Forward Seat	Jumping
Vertical seat; long leg slightly behind the girth; weight stretched down through heel; weight on crotch and sitting bones	Seat more toward forehand; shorter leg position; more weight in thighs, knees, heels	Seat out of saddle; short leg position on the girth; no weight in seat— all in thighs, knees, and heels
Center of gravity slightly toward hindquarters because of collected movements	Center of gravity slightly toward forehand due to extended frame	Center of gravity toward forehand due to extended frame over jump
Upper body vertical over hips	Upper body inclined slightly forward, more weight on crotch	Upper body inclined forward
Hands carried slightly in front of the withers	Hands above and slightly in front of the withers, reins shorter	Hands toward crest of neck; reins shorter to maintain contact
Approximately 90-degree angle between horse's neck and rider's upper body	Angle between horse's neck and rider's upper body slightly decreased	Angle between horse's neck and rider's upper body decreased because of forward inclination of upper-body position

the saddle, it also reduces the rider's effectiveness in achieving maximum use of the aids. Riders must work in balanced seats until they can coordinate their aids and achieve collection before reducing the aids at their disposal by shortening the stirrups and removing the seat from the saddle when jumping.

The same principles of balance previously explained apply to the forward seat as well as the balanced seat. The chief difference in the forward seat when working on the flat is the length of the stirrup and the slightly forward inclina-

tion of the upper body at a posting trot and canter.

Riders should practice riding in the forward seat at all three gaits, performing school movements and transitions until they become comfortable in the new position. At first riders may have difficulty applying leg aids effectively with the shortened leg position. Observe the students' equitation carefully to be sure that they do not form undesirable habits.

Use of the forward seat indicates to the observer that horse and rider will be negotiating uneven footing or going over

Fig. 74A. *Forward seat, posting trot. Note the levelness of the rider and the slight forward inclination of the upper body that accompanies the posting trot.*

Fig. 74B. Forward seat, three-point contact. As opposed to a balanced seat (dressage) saddle, a forward-seat saddle positions the rider toward the forehand of the horse. At the canter during flat work the upper body is angled slightly forward, the seat remains in the saddle to push the horse forward, and the stirrups are approximately two holes shorter than for the balanced seat, thus increasing the bend in the rider's knee.

Fig. 75. Forward seat, two-point contact, jump position. In jump position the rider's weight is dropped into the knees, thighs, and feet. The seat is removed from the saddle to allow the horse freedom to use his back when going over obstacles. In contrast to the basic position used on the flat, there is an increased angle in the rider's hips and knee.

obstacles. Therefore, a rider must begin to think "forward and over," rather than "sit back and collect." A major difference in philosophy has now been encountered. As soon as students are able to control their horses' performance and exhibit correct equitation in forward seat, two-point contact should be introduced.

TWO-POINT CONTACT

When riding in two-point contact, the rider lifts the seat out of the saddle, removing the weight from the horse's back and placing it down into the thighs, knees, and heels. The upper body is inclined slightly forward, allowing the balance point to shift toward the fore-hand, further unburdening the horse's

back and hindquarters. In this position the rider's only two points of contact with the horse are the legs.

Before students begin working over small obstacles or uneven terrain, let them practice riding in two-point contact on the flat to help strengthen their legs and attain proper balance at each gait.

To achieve the correct upper-body position for the jump position, the rider begins a rising trot, posts up, and holds the up position.

Fig. 76. A hand on the mane helps the rider maintain the correct position until sufficient balance and leg muscles have been developed.

ARENA EXERCISES

Two-Point Contact

When practicing two-point contact, have each student tie a knot in the reins and carry them in the outside hand while holding onto the mane about two-thirds up the horse's neck to attain added support (fig. 76). This procedure prevents the student from hanging onto the horse's mouth. Have the students work on the rail this way at all three gaits.

At first the riders will need frequent rest periods because their leg muscles are unaccustomed to carrying their total weight. When the correct balance has been achieved and students no longer have to rely on the mane for support, have them practice school movements

in jump position and upward and downward transitions without sitting down in the saddle. Remind them that the aids and body language remain the same; only the position of the rider is different.

Common Problems

1. *Reins too long.* Demonstrate that, when the upper body is inclined forward, the angle between the rider's body and the horse's neck begins to close. As this angle decreases in size, the rider must shorten the reins to control the position of the horse's head and neck and maintain a straight line between the bit and the elbow.

2. *Incorrect position of the lower leg.* In jump position the lower leg is at the girth (fig. 77). Some riders tend to posi-

BILL CULBERTSON

Fig. 77. In jump position the lower leg remains at the girth.

tion the leg too far behind the girth because they have been told to "bring the lower leg back under the body" when riding in balanced seat. For a firm basis of support the leg must remain directly under the body regardless of the seat being used. As the upper body is inclined forward, the leg must also be pushed forward to remain a sufficient basis of support.

3. *Rider standing in the stirrups.* A rider may tend to stand in the stirrups instead of depending on the thighs and knees for support. Correct this tendency by having the rider roll up onto the thighs and drop the weight down into the knees and heels. To help prevent the problem, have the students work in the basic forward-seat position and practice two-point contact without stirrups as soon as they have achieved an adequate degree of balance.

When riding without stirrups, the student should pull the stirrup-leather buckle down about six inches from the bar and then cross the stirrups over the

horse's neck just in front of the withers. Adjusting the buckle to a lower position on the leather will prevent it from bunching under the rider's leg and allow the leg to remain in a comfortable and correct position.

4. *Loss of position.* When students begin riding in the forward-seat position without stirrups, they may tend to seek support by pinching with the knees, thus forcing the lower leg either to ride up or to fall too far to the rear. If the knees pinch in and the lower leg rides up, the rider's seat is pushed too far to the rear of the saddle. To correct faulty position, have the rider grasp the pommel with the inside hand and pull the crotch, thigh, and seat forward. The knees should be lowered to correct lower-leg position under the rider's body. Have the students correct their positions whenever necessary.

Longeing Horse and Rider

Longeing is the ideal way to instill balance in a rider without the worry of controlling the horse or unintentionally pulling on his mouth. Work students without stirrups or reins at the three basic gaits in both forward seat and jump position. To help prepare students for jumping, an excellent exercise is to have each rider incline the upper body forward and roll up onto the thighs and knees. Also have them do this exercise in reverse, each rider leaning backward, almost touching the horse's rump with the back of the head. Throughout the exercise the lower leg must remain in correct position under the body to provide maximum support.

ARENA EXERCISES

Longeing Without Stirrups

Practice suppling exercises without stirrups at a walk and trot to help students establish their balance. Have each rider tie a knot in the reins and place them on the horse's neck. Longeing exercises for work in forward seat should include:

1. Riding with one hand on the hip and the other hand on the head.
2. Riding with the inside hand in the small of the back.
3. Posting without stirrups to help loosen thigh muscles.

Use of Ground Poles

Ground poles may be randomly scattered about the arena to accustom riders to going over easy obstacles. When students have become familiar with going over a simple pole, ground poles can be placed along the rail, on the centerline, or across the diagonal. Adequate space—at least five trot strides—should remain between

each pole (the normal length of a trot stride ranges from 4 feet 3 inches to 4 feet 10 inches, depending on the horse). The exercise begins with students riding in the forward seat at a posting trot. Alternate the posting trot with the jump position to allow practice in both seats. Alternating between the two seats also permits students to rest their leg muscles. The following exercises, performed at the trot over ground obstacles, will increase rider balance and strengthen lower legs in both the forward-seat and the jump positions.

Chute Exercises

An excellent way to help students increase their balance in forward seat and two-point contact is to assemble a chute along one side of the arena fence. Cavalletti are ideal for this purpose. First, place two cavalletti or ground poles on the track with one end next to the arena wall. The poles should be approximately 12 feet 9 inches apart (fig. 78). At this spacing the horse will trot over the first pole, take two trot strides, and then trot over the second pole. If the poles are set a little too close and the horse hits them as he trots over, separate them farther (see Appendix I for cavalletti spacing). Additional cavalletti are then placed parallel to the arena fence at the end of the ground poles to make a chute. These cavalletti are used at their tallest height and extend past the ground poles on both ends approximately 10 feet. If cavalletti are not available, barrels and poles can be arranged as one side of the chute.

In working riders through a chute, it is imperative that riders remain spaced well apart—that no rider enters the chute until the rider in front of him is completely out. If a horse stops in the middle of the chute and a second rider is following close behind, an accident may result. If a rider approaches the chute before the horse in front has finished, the approach-

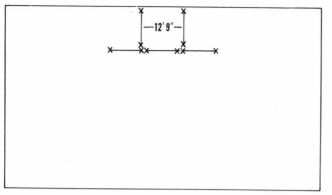

Fig. 78. Basic
ground-pole
chute exercise.

ing rider should turn away, circle, and then proceed when the chute is clear.

To prepare for these exercises, have each rider tie a knot in the reins and carry them loosely in the outside hand. If the riders are performing an exercise without using hands, the reins are placed on the horse's neck. In a no-reins exercise the rider is to hold the reins until after entering the chute. Perform each exercise at least twice from each direction. Do not exceed thirty minutes' total time in using the chute. Comment on each student's equitation after the work; the chute exercise is an excellent means of providing individual attention.

As students progress in ability, another ground pole may be added up to a maximum of four. As additional poles are used, the chute must be lengthened to allow ten feet on each end beyond the pole area. It is essential that all poles have the same spacing between them during elementary work. Add more than two poles as soon as students have become accustomed to chute exercises. Throughout all exercises encourage the students to look straight ahead. Use a designated object to prevent riders from looking down. Looking down must be avoided, since dropping the head can greatly alter a rider's balance as obstacles become more difficult.

Introduce the following progressive

trotting exercises for work in a chute. Forward-seat exercises should precede exercises performed in jump position.

Forward Seat—Posting Trot.

1. Reins held loosely in outside hand.
2. No reins, hands on hips or one hand on hip and the other hand on top of head.
3. No reins, no stirrups, arms extended out at sides.
4. No reins, no stirrups, eyes closed.

Jump Position—Two Point Contact. The riders approach the chute at a posting trot and assume the jump position before entering the chute:

1. Outside hand on reins, inside hand grasping mane two-thirds up the horse's neck for support.
2. Outside hand on hip, inside hand on mane.
3. Both hands on hips.
4. Arms extended at the sides.
5. Inside hand on mane, outside hand on hip, no stirrups.
6. No reins, no stirrups, hands at the sides.
7. No reins, no stirrups, hands on hips, eyes closed.

Down the Centerline

A trotting exercise that can be performed over ground poles by placing obstacles

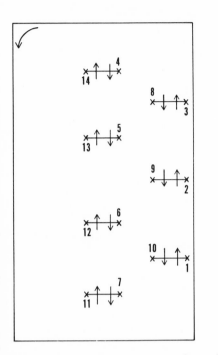

Fig. 79. A cavalletti exercise performed at the trot.

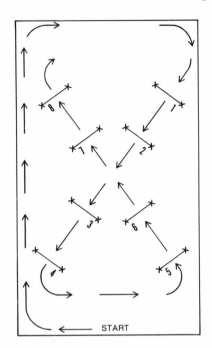

Fig. 80. A cavalletti exercise utilizing arena diagonals.

along one side of the arena and on the centerline. Four or more trot strides separate each pole. This exercise, shown in figure 79, begins on the left rein in forward seat at a posting trot: 1–3, posting trot, forward seat; down the centerline; 4–7, jump position; track right; 8–10, posting trot, jumping position; up the centerline; 11–14, jump position; track left, posting trot; return to number 1 and repeat sequence if desired.

Across the Diagonal

To execute a more advanced trot exercise, place ground poles across both diagonals leaving the center portion of each diagonal clear. The rail of the arena also remains clear. The space between ground poles will be shorter than that used with poles on the centerline, but at least one or two trot strides should remain between the poles. The number of trot strides

between each pole is determined by the size of the arena and the need to keep the center portion of the diagonals clear of obstacles. Two trot strides between the poles should be sufficient for this exercise. If two strides are to be taken between the poles, they should be set 12 feet 9 inches apart to start and the space adjusted as needed.

In the exercise shown in figure 80, the riders begin on the rail, tracking right, in forward seat at a posting trot. When crossing the diagonals, they maintain jump position. A posting trot is used on the rail.

This exercise is executed in a figure-eight pattern, the riders continually crossing the diagonal, posting across a short side of the arena, crossing the diagonal in jump position, riding across a short end in a posting trot, and so on. The instructor should designate a leader, and the other riders should follow a horse's length apart to avoid confusion. Horses are kept in a file, and each rider follows the horse in front. This exercise should be performed in both directions.

As the riders' proficiency in maintaining the jump position becomes obvious, the ground-pole series can be increased to three poles before the center of the diagonal is reached, and the space between them can be shortened to allow only one trot stride between the ground obstacles. Spacing to allow one trot stride between two ground obstacles begins at 8 feet 6 inches and is lengthened according to the horse's stride.

Cavalletti Square

A cavalletti or a ground-pole square can be used to practice straight lines and a bend. In the exercise shown in figure 81, poles are placed across from each other at least 12 feet 9 inches apart.

This exercise is performed individually first at a posting trot and then in jump position. A rider circles in front of the first obstacle, comes through the center of the circle, and trots straight for the center of the first ground pole. After trotting over the second pole, the rider turns left, bending the horse through the turn, and then rides a straight line through the third and fourth poles and either halts or turns right and repeats the exercise, at the discretion of the instructor.

The cavalletti or ground-pole square is an excellent exercise to increase the riders' ability to ride a straight line and then a curved line, while maintaining forward-seat or jump position. Review with the students the body language for riding a straight line and the aids for a correct bend. Nothing in the body language changes except the position of the rider's seat and the slight forward inclination of the upper body.

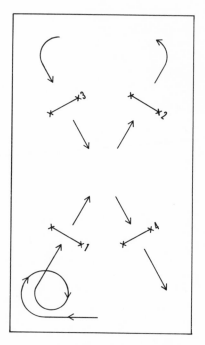

Fig. 81. Cavalletti-square exercise.

WORK IN THE OPEN

Work the forward-seat and jump positions in open fields or pastures. If small banks are available, encourage students to walk and trot up and down the banks, maintaining the jump position. Demonstrate the proper position and then observe each rider individually. When riding up a bank, students may hold onto the mane to help maintain their position up and out of the saddle. They must look where they are going and not concentrate on the horse or look down at the ground.

In riding down a small incline, the novice rider tends to incline the upper body too far forward, thus getting ahead of the horse's movement. The rider must maintain a balanced position over the horse's center of gravity, no matter what activity is being performed. Also check for correct lower-leg position. If the upper body is positioned too far forward, the lower leg will most likely be too far back. With sufficient weight pushed down the leg and into the heel, the rider pushes the leg up underneath so that the lower leg is positioned on the girth.

Summary

Intermediate equitation acquaints riders with a flexible seat—the knowledge "when to use what type of seat." The students first work in the balanced seat or dressage seat, where they have full use of the aids at their disposal before shortening their base of support by shortening their stirrups to ride in forward seat. Then the two-point-contact or jump position is introduced, which further reduced the rider's support apparatus by taking the seat out of the saddle and placing all support in the thighs, knees, and heels.

Modification of each seat is dictated by the activity being performed and the terrain being covered. The rider strives to achieve an independent, well-balanced, adaptable seat so that the position can be easily adjusted to remain in common equilibrium with the horse, whatever type of work is being performed.

When students have mastered this level of riding, they will be able to ride their horses using body language and will understand the purpose of the aids and the need to coordinate them. They will be able to ride smoothly at all three gaits and work a horse in the proper shape and will understand the displacement of the horse's center of gravity at collected and extended paces. With this introduction to forward-seat riding, students are ready for basic cavalletti and jump work. Dressage training should be continued at the advanced-equitation level to help maintain the horse's suppleness, obedience, and willingness to move forward.

Part Three

Advanced
Equitation

Chapter 7

Cavalletti Work

Students should now possess sufficient equestrian skills and muscular coordination to allow them to progress to cavalletti work, jumping a small course and lateral movements. The interrelationships of dressage and jumping will become apparent as students begin riding a small course composed of straight and curved lines. Advanced equitation is based on the basic cavalletti work the students have just completed. Now they begin working with the principle of riding "forward and over" an obstacle. In all work over obstacles students are required to wear hard hats with straps secured and are encouraged to wear gloves to prevent their hands from slipping on the reins.

Basic Cavalletti Work

POLES

Ten or twelve cavalletti will prove invaluable instructional tools. They are relatively easy to build (construction plans are detailed in Appendix J). Three heights are needed: (1) ground pole— right at the ground or just slightly above, (2) trot height—six inches off the ground, and (3) canter height—eighteen inches off the ground.

Place three or four poles at trot-pole height randomly about the arena on the rail. Have the students ride at a posting trot over the poles to become accustomed to going over obstacles that are higher than ground level. When the riders can negotiate the single trot poles, set up a simple sequence of trot poles.

Space the trot poles approximately 4 feet 3 inches to 4 feet 6 inches apart, depending on the horses' length of stride. During elementary exercises place trot poles along the arena wall to keep horses from running out in one direction. Additional cavalletti can be used in constructing a simple chute (fig. 82).

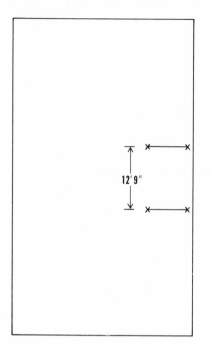

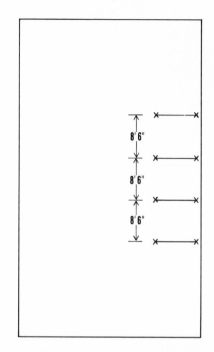

Fig. 82. Basic trot-pole work begins
with sufficient space between each pole
to allow students time to think and
react to a new situation.

Fig. 83A. As the riders' proficiency
increases, the number of poles is
increased, and the space between the
poles is shortened.

ARENA EXERCISES

Basic Exercise

The basic trot-pole exercise begins with
two poles at trot-pole height set approximately 12 feet 9 inches apart. The horse
is to trot over a pole, take two trot strides,
and trot over the next pole. Have the students perform basic balance exercises
over the poles. As soon as possible, a
third pole and then a fourth can be added
to the sequence, and the spacing can be
shortened so that only one trot stride is
taken between each pole. Spacing for this
exercise, "over-stride-over," starts at
8 feet 6 inches and can be adjusted according to the horses' stride.

The exercise is next performed in both
directions. A posting trot in both forward-seat and the jump position is used.

As soon as possible, remove the cavalletti
forming the chute to prevent students
from depending on it to keep the horses
moving straight. Horse and rider must
strive to cross the center of each obstacle
(fig. 83A).

Trot-Pole Variations

The following variations of trot-pole
exercises are practiced in both forward-
seat and jump positions. The sequence is
intentional to allow students to build
confidence and increase their skill.

Open Stride (fig. 84). Cavalletti 1 to 3
have two trot strides between the poles;
spacing is approximately 12 feet 9 inches.
Cavalletti 4 and 5 have no trot strides
between them; spacing is approximately
4 feet 3 inches to 4 feet 6 inches. Caval-

spaced out, follow the horse in front, and never enter a series of cavalletti before the rider in front is completely clear.

Across the Diagonal (fig. 85). Spacing is approximately 8 feet 6 inches to allow for one trot stride between the poles. Have the students perform the exercise on the left rein, executing a change of rein after crossing the diagonal. Have them ride a straight line through the cavalletti and bend their horses through the corners.

On the Rail (figs. 86A and 86B). Spacing is approximately 4 feet 3 inches to allow for no trot step between the poles. Students should work large and change the rein up the centerline to achieve the change of direction.

On the Centerline (fig. 87). Spacing between poles 1, 2, and 3 is approximately 4 feet 3 inches, with no trot strides in between. Two trot strides follow with the distance approximately 12 feet 9 inches. Cavalletti 4 and 5 have no trot strides between them. A change of rein may be executed when riders come up and down the centerline and over the cavalletti.

The exercises become progressively more difficult, demanding more skill in both horse and rider. When the crutch of the chute is removed, students must ride a straight line through the center of the cavalletti series, bend their horses through the corner, and continue on the prescribed course either in jump position or at a posting trot as directed by the instructor.

The instructor must carefully watch each rider's position to make sure that the upper body does not incline too far forward or remain too vertical, that the lower leg is on the girth, and that the reins are short enough to maintain con-

Fig. 83B. The instructor should observe students from behind to see that they are remaining squarely positioned on the horse. An imaginary horizontal line should pass through both shoulders and through the elbows, the hips, the knees, and the ankles. This rider's right knee and lower leg are dropped owing to the lowering of the horse's right quarter as he trots through the cavalletti series.

letti 6 and 7 have one stride between them; spacing is approximately 8 feet 6 inches.

Before the exercise begins, ask the students to identify visually the number of trot strides between the poles. This will help to train the eye to prepare riders to read a jump course. Riders must stay

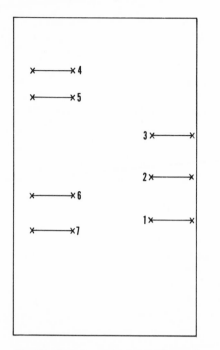

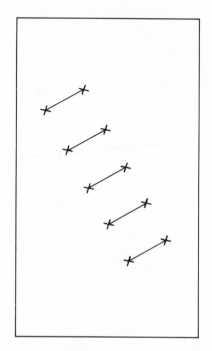

Fig. 84. Exercises that vary the striding over cavalletti provide a challenge for both horse and rider.

Fig. 85. Trot poles across the diagonal. Students should ride a straight line through the center of a cavalletti series, with a change of rein executed after they cross the diagonal.

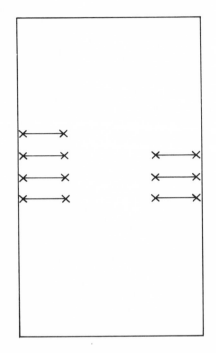

Fig. 86A. Riding a straight line through the center of a cavalletti series helps students learn to emphasize the use of the proper aids.

Fig. 86B. Trot poles on the rail. Cavalletti work encourages the horse to maintain a round shape on the flat, and its suppling effect on the horse's back aids in the proper execution of the sitting trot.

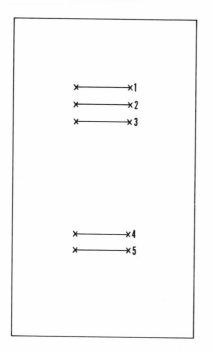

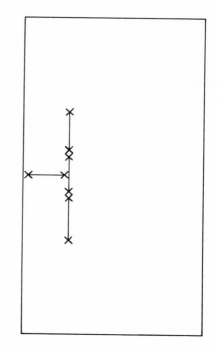

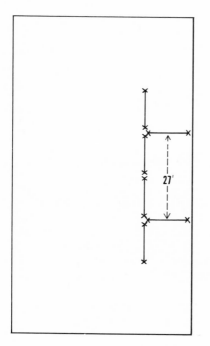

Fig. 87 (top left). Setting trot poles with varied spacing helps develop the concentration of both horse and rider.

Fig. 88 (top right). For some riders the first cantering pole may appear an awesome obstacle.

Fig. 89 (left). A chute with two cantering poles set with two canter strides between them allows students to develop the feel of a cantering-pole series.

tact with the horse's mouth. Also check to see that the rider's hands are carried approximately one-third up the neck and that a straight line remains from the bit all the way through the rider's hand and wrist to the elbow.

CANTERING POLES

When introducing all exercises, have riders tie a knot in the reins and carry them in the outside hand. The inside hand holds the mane one-third to one-half the way up the horse's neck to help maintain jump position. When riders can maintain balance and control in this position, each hand should be placed firmly on top of the crest approximately one-third the way up the horse's neck (crest release). This position allows the rider to follow the motion of the horse's head and neck when going over a jump without losing contact with the reins and bumping the horse in the mouth. The crest release is assumed five to six strides *before* a cavalletti series is begun. In an over-over no-stride sequence place cantering poles 9 to 12 feet apart, depending on the horse's length of stride.

ARENA EXERCISES

Single Cavalletti

Set one cavalletti pole on the rail and another in a chute. Have each student individually canter over the pole with a knot tied in the reins and the reins carried in the outside hand. Have the rider place the inside hand on the mane for added support (figs. 88 and 89).

Next add a second pole, approximately 27 feet from the first. Have the students take two canter strides between the poles, in the sequence over-stride-stride-over. Now add a third pole, again 27 feet from

the second pole. The sequence is now over-stride-stride-over-stride-stride-over. Have the students say the sequence as they canter the poles. Figuring out the puzzle and saying it aloud helps them establish the feel of the obstacle course.

Chute Variation

The same exercise is repeated, but with the spacing altered so that the horse takes only one canter stride between the poles (figs. 90A and 90B). The students should figure out the puzzle and say, "Over-stride-over," as they ride the sequence.

When the riders have developed a feel for going over the cantering cavalletti, use balance exercises with one stride between the poles. Remove the cavalletti forming the side of the chute and have them return the reins to both hands and assume the crest-release position. Repeat the exercise.

Trot and Canter-Pole Exercises

The combination series is as follows: (1) cavalletti 1 to 3, cantering poles, one stride between, (2) cavalletti 4 and 5, trot poles, no stride between, and (3) cavalletti 6 and 7, trot poles, one trot stride between (fig. 91).

Bounce (No-Stride) Exercises

Again setting up a chute, place two cavalletti 9 to 12 feet apart (fig. 92). This is a bounce—that is, there is no canter stride between. Have the riders say, "Over-over." Add a third cantering pole when the students' proficiency warrants. The students should say the bounce sequence, "Over-over-over."

Next, remove the cavalletti forming one side of the chute so that the students must use their aids to keep the horse straight and prevent him from running out.

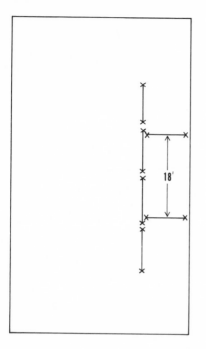

Fig. 90A (left). Balance exercises performed in a chute play an important role developing the riders' confidence and agility. Without balance and confidence it is impossible for students to jump larger obstacles.

Fig. 90B (below). Cantering cavalletti. The rider remains in jump position throughout the cavalletti exercise. An advanced rider will be able to maintain contact with the horse's mouth without pulling on the reins because of balance and development of leg muscles. Note the look of forward motion and the attentive attitude of both the horse and the rider.

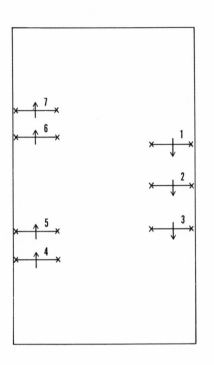

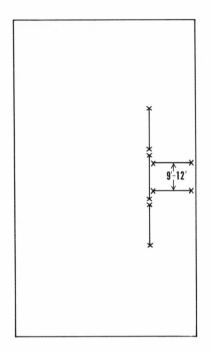

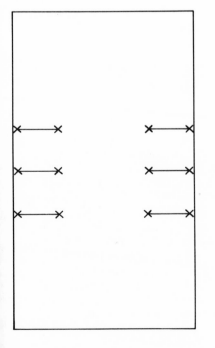

Fig. 91 (top left). A combination of cantering poles and trot poles tests the rider's timing and ability to use the proper aids to bend the horse through the corner and keep him moving on a straight line through the series of obstacles.

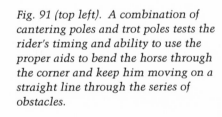

Fig. 92 (top right). A no-stride obstacle is called a bounce.

Fig. 93 (left). Cavalletti can be combined for more difficult exercises that call for a change of rein or a simple change of lead between obstacle series.

Advanced No-Stride Exercises

Along the long sides of the arena place two sets of three cantering cavalletti with no strides between (fig. 93). A change of rein with a simple change of lead can be executed up and down the centerline. When several students are performing this exercise together, adequate space between horses is imperative. Do not allow a student to enter the series until the rider in front is clear. If a rider is too close, have the rider turn away and circle until the series is clear.

Across the Diagonal

Place cantering poles across the diagonal with one canter stride between (fig. 94). Shorten the space between the cantering poles so that they become a series of bounces. A maximum of four cantering poles may be used, depending on the riders' proficiency and the size of the arena. Remember that a rider should trot into the series, canter over the poles, and then trot *before* reaching the corner of the arena. The purpose of this exercise is to teach students to ride a straight line through the middle of a series without depending on an arena wall to keep the horse on the proper course.

Combination Series

Poles 1, 2, and 3 are set at canter height; poles 1 and 2 have one canter stride between them; between poles 2 and 3 is a bounce (fig. 95). Have the students drop to a trot. Cavalletti 4 and 5 are trot poles set with one stride between them.

Make the transition from canter to trot with the riders remaining in jump position. The riders should first read the puzzle, saying to the instructor, "Over–stride–over–over–transition-to-trot–over–stride–over."

Advanced Combination Series

Poles 1 to 4 are set at canter height; all are bounces (fig. 96); poles 5 to 7 are trot poles, no stride between, poles 8 and 9 are cantering poles, one stride between. The students should read the puzzle and say, "Over-over-over-over-trot-over-over-over-canter-over-stride-over."

Many other sequential patterns for cantering poles and a combination of cantering poles and trot poles can be used. Be creative in designing safe and effective exercises. Care must be taken to maintain proper spacing between the cavalletti. Improper spacing will cause horses to hit the obstacles and stumble or fall.

Work over cavalletti should constitute no more than a thirty- to forty- minute segment of a lesson. Horses and riders will tire physically and mentally, and school horses can sour with overuse. Intersperse cavalletti lessons with work on the flat. Working fifteen minutes in the open or on a long rein in a field at the end of the lesson provides a relaxing atmosphere in which to end the session.

Cavalletti Courses

Cavalletti can be used in a simple jump course. Have the students trot the course first to be sure they can ride the straight lines and curves correctly and remain in a balanced position. Then adjust the cavalletti to canter height and have them ride the course at the canter.

To ride the course, each rider canters a circle in front of the first jump, determining the direction of the circle and corresponding lead by the direction of the first turn on the course. Throughout the remainder of the course have the riders execute a simple change of lead with as few trot steps as possible during elementary training periods. Keep the course open with ample room between

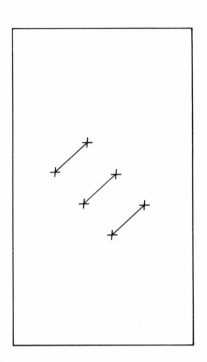

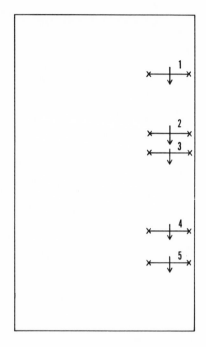

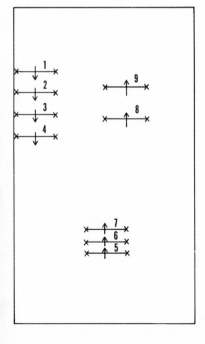

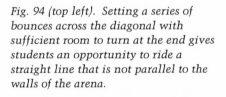

Fig. 94 (top left). Setting a series of bounces across the diagonal with sufficient room to turn at the end gives students an opportunity to ride a straight line that is not parallel to the walls of the arena.

Fig. 95 (top right). Cavalletti striding puzzle. Riders should always verbalize the cavalletti "puzzle," reading the striding before negotiating the obstacles.

Fig. 96 (left). Advanced cavalletti striding puzzle. Teaching students to think ahead, read, and study an obstacle course before attempting it is an important part of their education.

obstacles to allow students time to think and to position their horses correctly between fences.

The following sample courses should be used in the sequence in which they appear. One canter circle before beginning the course and one canter circle on finishing the course are permissible. As with trot obstacles, adjust the distance between cantering obstacles according to the horses being used and the average length of stride. A simple change of lead should be executed following obstacles placed across a diagonal.

ELEMENTARY COURSES USING SINGLE CAVALLETTI

Course to the Left

In the course shown in figure 97, the riders begin by circling on the left lead, since the first turn in the course is to the left. Have the riders execute a simple change of lead between cavalletti 4 and 5. The course shown in figure 98 calls for more control and more consistent use of the aids. Simple in design, the course is more difficult to ride.

Course to the Right

When riding the course shown in figure 99, the rider circles to the right, since the first turn in the course is in that direction.

COMPOUND CAVALLETTI OBSTACLES

Riders must learn how to jump wider obstacles before jumping higher ones. Jumping low, wide obstacles gives them the opportunity to understand that a jump is simply another canter stride, only longer and wider. To provide wider jumps, place two cavalletti close together side by side (fig. 100).

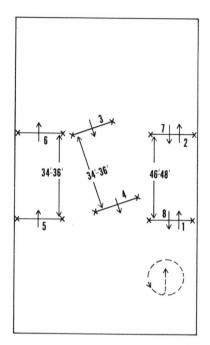

Fig. 97. Several cavalletti can be used to design an elementary obstacle course with simple turns.

When students can negotiate these obstacles on the rail and across the diagonal, add a third cavalletti (fig. 101). This low, spread jump helps the riders develop the feel for jumping. As obstacles become wider, the rider must lengthen the canter stride and allow the horse to reach forward. Bales of straw can also be used to make a safe jump (fig. 102). For more height place additional bales on top.

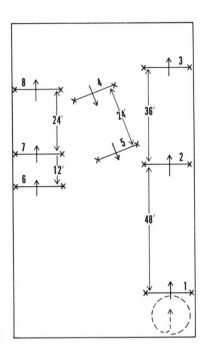

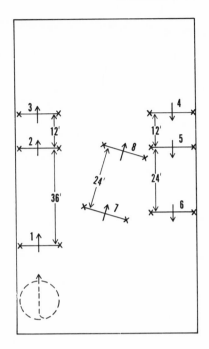

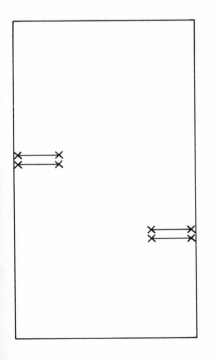

Fig. 98 (top left). Advanced cavalletti obstacle course. Properly designed, a cavalletti course gives students an opportunity to learn the feel of correct striding.

Fig. 99 (top right). Cavalletti course to the right. All courses are made up of only two elements: straight lines and curved lines.

Fig. 100 (left). Riders must learn to jump low, wide obstacles before negotiating high obstacles.

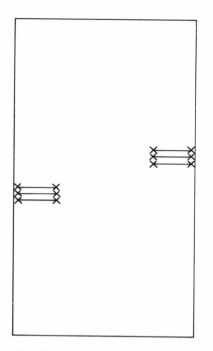

Fig. 101. To negotiate three-cavalletti spreads, the rider must lengthen the horse's stride and allow him to stretch forward.

JUMPING IN NATURAL TERRAIN

Students should now possess adequate skills to negotiate a small course set in natural terrain. Take advantage of small banks and ditches in a pasture and incorporate them into a small outdoor course. Inexpensive materials such as barrels, railroad ties, old tires, and wooden pallets can be assembled into obstacles of various heights and widths. All wood jumps must be strong and free of old nails and sharp edges (fig. 105).

LOW HOGBACK JUMPS

Cavalletti can be stacked together to make low hogback jumps. To make a low hogback, set two cavalletti next to each other at cantering-pole height and a third cavalletti on top at trot-pole height (fig. 103). As the proficiency of horse and rider increases, adjust the top element to cantering-pole height (fig. 104). After practicing over single hogbacks, students can ride simple courses with hogbacks replacing the single cavalletti. When hogbacks are used instead of single cavalletti, it is advisable to omit the bounce jumps and use a minimum of 24 feet, one stride, to replace the 10-to-12-foot bounce between fences.

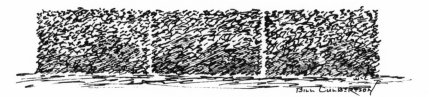

Fig. 102. Bales of straw are safe to jump and provide a basic wide obstacle.

Fig. 103. Low hogback jump.

Fig. 104. High hogback jump.

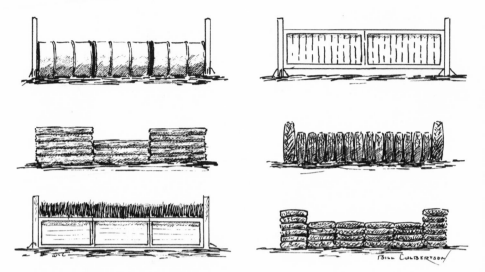

Fig. 105. *Inexpensive materials can make good jumps. Care must be taken to remove nails and other sharp objects that could cause injury to horse or rider.*

Chapter 8

Turn on the Haunches

In the discussion of the turn on the forehand (see Chapter 4) it was noted that the rider must take care not to override the turn; otherwise the horse may resist when asked to perform a turn on the haunches. This movement is the opposite of the turn on the forehand in that the forequarters are moved around the hindquarters. This turn helps make the horse's forehand light, because it requires the hindquarters to become the weight-bearing surface.

The turn on the haunches, executed at a medium walk, is a preparatory exercise for the pirouette, which is the same turn but performed at the collected walk. During the turn on the haunches the horse is expected to maintain the rhythm of the medium walk. The turning action is centered around the inside hind leg. During the turn the horse moves the forelegs and the outside hind leg around the inside hind leg. The inside hind leg acts as the center, but it should be lifted from the ground and returned to the same spot or slightly in front of the original spot. Placing the foot backward is a fault; placing the inside hindfoot slightly in front is acceptable. The inside hind leg should never assume an unmoving pivot position because that will cause the leg to twist. Impulsion, collection, and the rhythm of the medium walk must be maintained throughout the turn. The horse walks into the turn, performs the turn, and walks away from the turn all in the same distinct, rhythmic four-beat gait.

AIDS TO TURNING
ON THE HAUNCHES

As with all other movements, a half-halt calls the horse to attention before the turn is executed. The rider sits inward with more influence on the inside sitting bone and looks in the direction of travel.

When the rider looks in the direction of travel, the body will be correctly positioned for the turn. The rider's inside leg remains at the girth to maintain a slight bend. It can be brought into action more toward the rear if the inside hind foot resists movement and begins twisting. The inside rein defines the degree of bend and leads the horse around the inside hind leg. The outside rein and outside leg, positioned behind the girth, push the horse around the inside of the turn and prevent overbending through use of the outside unilateral aids. The rider's outside leg is also used behind the girth to prevent the haunches from falling out of the turn. If the horse fails to respond to the sideways pressure of the rider's outside leg, the whip may be lightly applied behind the rider's leg to reinforce the action. Explain to the students that they should always apply leg pressure first and follow with gentle taps of the whip. They are to think of the whip as an extension of the leg to reinforce the leg pressure. They should never use the whip as a *replacement* for the riders' own aids. The aids must be actively maintained until the horse has completed the turn and returns to the track.

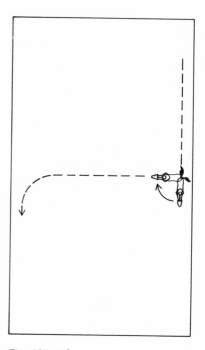

Fig. 106. *The quarter-turn is the first exercise used when teaching the turn on the haunches.*

ARENA EXERCISES

1. The basic exercise for the turn on the haunches begins from a simple quarter-turn (fig. 106). Each step can be performed individually until horse and rider know what is expected of them. To perform a quarter-turn on the haunches, the student rides down a long side of the arena, half-halts, applies the aids for the turn, and executes the turn step by step. This sequence reinforces the aids, helps the horse step correctly with the inside hind leg, and helps prevent the horse from stepping backward. He will have to pick up the inside hind leg each time

he performs a step as long as there is a definite halt between each step. The sequence should be: step-halt-step-halt, and so on. After the quarter-turn is completed, the student rides the horse across the arena, changes the rein, and repeats the exercise in the opposite direction.

2. Following the basic quarter-turn on the haunches, have the students practice a half-turn on the haunches, gradually reducing the size of the turn as the horse comes to understand the movement and becomes increasingly responsive to the aids (fig. 107). The rider must remember to maintain the aids and keep the legs active until the turn is completed.

Common Problems

1. *The horse pivots on the inside hind*

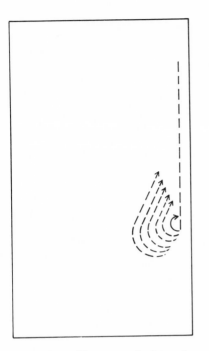

Fig. 107. Half-turn on the haunches.

3. *Impulsion is lacking.* Encourage the rider to use leg aids more actively.

4. *The horse backs during the turn.* Encourage the rider to increase leg aids to maintain impulsion and forward movement throughout the turn. Emphasize the use of the outside leg to hold the hindquarters. The rider must not pull back on the reins. Have the rider practice the quarter-turn on the haunches step by step, maintaining active forward movement throughout the turn.

5. *The haunches swing out of place.* The rider must increase the use of the outside leg behind the girth to hold the haunches in place.

6. *The horse's movement lacks a rhythmic four-beat gait.* The rider has failed to maintain sufficient impulsion throughout the turn. Have the rider practice the quarter-turn on the haunches until the horse maintains rhythm and the rider successfully coordinates the aids.

7. *The rider's driving aids are insufficient.* The rider must increase the use of leg aids and maintain them in the correct position throughout the turn.

8. *The rider is positioned to the outside of the saddle.* The rider's position should be readjusted to the inside of the saddle. Have the rider lower the heel and put more weight in the inside stirrup; the outside stirrup may be dropped as an added aid to prevent the rider from returning to the incorrect position.

leg. Have the rider move the inside leg toward the rear of the horse and use it actively to increase impulsion.

2. *The bend in the horse's body is insufficient.* Emphasize to the rider the importance of inside leg pressure at the girth. Check to be sure the reins allow the horse's head and neck to be positioned correctly.

Chapter 9

Lateral Movements

Lateral movements are advanced suppling exercises to increase the horse's over-all ability to perform in the dressage arena or on the hunt field. The introduction to lateral movements began with leg yielding, the horse being pushed sideways and forward while bent slightly away from the direction of travel. As soon as the horse understands the rider's leg aids pushing sideways, the lateral work should begin. With the exception of the shoulder-in, the following lateral movements require the horse to look in the direction of travel.

Shoulder-In

Because it is the basis of all other lateral work, the *shoulder-in* is considered the most important exercise on two tracks. During the shoulder-in the horse's forehand is moved inside the track while the haunches remain on the track. The horse is bent around the rider's inside leg and bent away from the direction of travel at a 30- to 33-degree angle from the wall (fig. 108). The horse's shoulder is in front of the inside hindquarter. The inside foreleg crosses over the outside foreleg, and the inside hind leg moves in front of the outside hind leg and diagonally up under the body. During the shoulder-in, the hind legs carry a great deal of weight, thus freeing the horse's shoulders and front legs to step forward.

AIDS TO SHOULDER-IN

The rider's inside leg is used at the girth to maintain the bend and to cause the inside foreleg to step over the outside foreleg and the inside hind leg to step well under the body. The rider should step down into the inside stirrup and lower the inside hip and knee to maximize the use of the inside leg. The out-

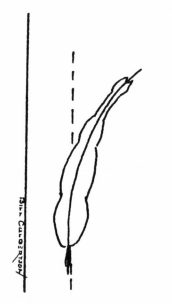 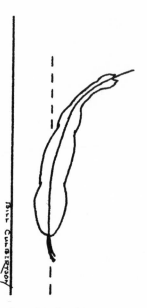

Fig. 108. Bending during shoulder-in exercise. Left: *During the shoulder-in exercise the horse should bend uniformly from poll to tail.* Right: *Too much bend in the head and neck positions the horse incorrectly to perform the movement.*

side leg is placed behind the girth to prevent the haunches from falling out.

The inside rein defines the degree of bend. The outside rein limits the bend and leads the horse in the direction of travel. It also helps control the horse's balance and degree of collection.

During the shoulder-in exercise the rider's shoulders remain parallel with the shoulders of the horse. The rider's weight is placed more toward the inside of the horse, and the inside leg and inside sitting bone push the horse to the outside rein, which leads the horse along the wall at the desired angle.

ARENA EXERCISES

At first, encourage the riders to be satisfied with a few steps of shoulder-in. When the horse responds correctly, have them ride a few steps of shoulder-in and then straighten the horse and ride forward

on a single track. This sequence not only rewards the horse but also helps him renew impulsion. When the students understand the mechanics of riding a shoulder-in at the walk, they may ride the exercise at a collected trot. The latter gait provides more impulsion. The shoulder-in is never ridden at the canter.

Shoulder-In from a Circle

Next have the students ride a circle next to the long side of the arena (fig. 109). Encourage them to think of the circle as an aid to help define the horse's bend and give the rider an opportunity to regulate the pace. While riding the circle, the rider presses down on the inside heel to be sure he is not riding to the outside of the saddle. As the horse again approaches the long side, the rider maintains sufficient collection and increases the bend to bring the forehand inside the track of the hindquarters. On

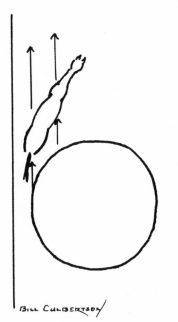

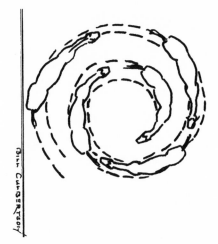

Fig. 109. Shoulder-in from a circle.

Fig. 111. Spiral-out exercise using the shoulder-in position. The horse should never be overdrilled on a lateral movement. It is the rider's responsibility to know when the horse has had enough. Difficult exercises should be interspersed with work on a straight line.

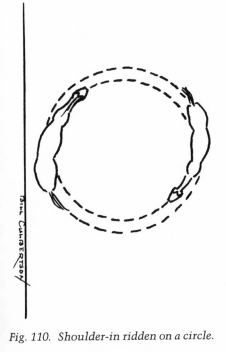

Fig. 110. Shoulder-in ridden on a circle.

reaching the long side, the rider half-halts and then pushes the horse on a straight line down the long side of the arena, riding a tangent to the circle. Care must be taken not to overbend the horse's head and neck. Use a strong outside rein and leg to correct this problem. The rider's inside leg is used at the girth to maintain the bend and forward movement. The outside leg is used behind the girth to control the position of the haunches. If the correct shoulder-in position is lost, have the rider return the horse to the circle and begin again.

Shoulder-In on a Circle

It is possible to ride a circle in the shoulder-in position (fig. 110). When the circle has been established and the pace regulated, the horse's forehand is moved inside the track, and the circle is ridden in the shoulder-in position. If the correct position is lost, have the student ride the circle on a single track and quietly reestablish the shoulder-in position.

Shoulder-In in a Spiral-Out

Shoulder-in can also be performed during a spiral-out exercise. First, have the student ride a series of gradually smaller circles on a single track (fig. 111). Then have the rider gradually increase the size of the circles by moving the horse outward in the shoulder-in position. At the intermediate level leg yielding was used to spiral-out. Now the basic position is adjusted to become the shoulder-in. When the students understand the mechanics of this exercise, have them spiral-in at the trot on a single track and spiral-out on two tracks, using the shoulder-in.

Common Problems

1. *The horse fails to maintain rhythm and forward motion.* The rider must increase the use of leg aids. Check to be sure the horse is not overbent.

2. *The horse is not uniformly bent from poll to tail.* Check the rider's rein length (too short or too long) and increase or decrease the bend in the horse's body so that the bend in the head and neck, defined through the position of the reins and the bend in the horse's body, is the same.

3. *The horse's shoulder is not taken far enough off the track, and the hind-quarters are allowed to swing out.* The rider should lead the forehand more off the track and apply additional outside leg pressure behind the girth to keep the hindquarters on the track.

4. *The horse's position is slowly allowed to straighten, and the shoulder returns to the track.* The rider must maintain the proper aids and bend in the horse throughout the exercise.

5. *The movement is not uniformly executed on both reins.* Because all horses are naturally more supple on one side than on the other, the rider should practice all suppling exercises and shoulder-in exercises in both directions until the horse has achieved a uniform degree of suppleness and balance when working in both directions.

Half-Pass

In performing the half-pass, the horse moves obliquely forward across the diagonal (fig. 112). He is bent around the rider's inside leg, but only to the slight degree that the rider can see the outside corner of the horse's inside eye. The horse looks in the direction of travel and maintains the rhythm and balance of the gait required. The half-pass is first practiced at the walk and later can be ridden at the trot and the canter. In this movement, as in all other lateral move-

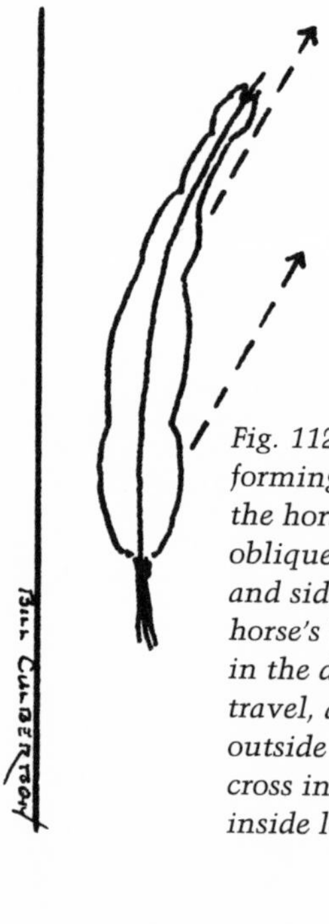

Fig. 112. In performing a half-pass, the horse moves obliquely forward and sideways. The horse's body is bent in the direction of travel, and the outside legs pass and cross in front of the inside legs.

ments, the hindquarters must never be allowed to lead. If the hindquarters assume a more advanced position than that of the forehand, a serious fault has been committed.

AIDS TO HALF-PASS

When executing the half-pass, the rider thinks "forward and sideways." Forward movement must always be the first consideration, because this movement is necessary to establish impulsion and the rhythm of the gait. Impulsion and rhythm must then be maintained during the sideways movement.

Have the rider perform a half-halt and then sit inward in the saddle and place more emphasis on the inside sitting bone to help move the horse in the direction of travel. The inside rein defines the degree of bend, while contact on the outside rein limits the bend. Sufficient contact must be maintained on the outside rein to prevent the horse from overbending the head and neck. The rider's outside leg is used behind the girth to push the horse obliquely forward and sideways. The inside leg remains at the girth to maintain impulsion and the proper degree of bend in the horse's body.

ARENA EXERCISES

1. The horse is ridden down the long side of the arena. A half-halt calls him to attention, and he makes a large half-turn. Upon reaching the diagonal line back to the track, the rider again calls the horse to attention with a half-halt, and the half-pass is executed (fig. 113). A few steps before reaching the track, the rider straightens the horse, rides forward on a single track, and executes a change of rein. The rider repeats the exercise on the other rein.

2. Shoulder-in is performed along a

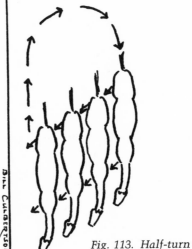

Fig. 113. Half-turn and half-pass.

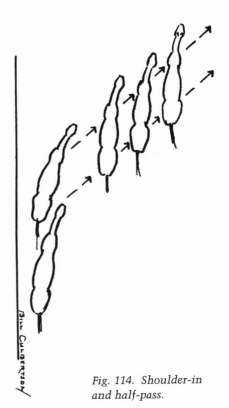

Fig. 114. Shoulder-in and half-pass.

long side to help establish the horse's bend. At a designated point the rider executes a half-halt, changes the pressure from the inside leg to the outside leg, and pushes the horse diagonally toward the centerline (fig. 114). If the horse fails to maintain the proper position, the rider moves him forward and quietly repeats the exercise.

When riding both exercises, it is important for students to remember never to start the half-pass movement directly from a corner, because this encourages the haunches to lead the forehand. Too much sideways influence of the rider's outside leg coupled with insufficient impulsion and lack of rein aids also cause the haunches to lead.

Common Problems

1. *The haunches tend to lead the movement.* The rider should increase impulsion and forward movement while reducing outside leg influence to push the horse sideways. Check the position of the reins and the bend in the horse to determine whether the horse is in the proper position to perform the movement correctly.

2. *The horse is too straight or incorrectly bent.* The rider should increase the use of the inside leg at the girth and the outside leg behind the girth to encourage the bend in the direction of travel. Check the rein aids to be sure the horse is looking in the direction of movement.

3. *The horse lacks impulsion.* The rider must use more active leg aids and concentrate on establishing sufficient forward movement before moving the horse sideways.

4. *The rider is positioned too far to the outside of the saddle.* Have the rider drop the outside stirrup, place more weight in the inside stirrup, lower the heel, and sit inward in the direction of travel. Drop-

ping the outside stirrup eliminates the rider's base of support on the outside of the horse and makes it easier to place additional weight in the inside stirrup, thus correctly adjusting the position to the inside and in the direction of travel.

5. *The rider collapses the inside hip.* Ask the student either to "raise the inside shoulder" or to "lower the outside shoulder." When the rider's shoulders maintain a level position, the hip will not be collapsed.

Haunches-In (Travers)

When performing *haunches-in*, the horse moves along the rail with his head positioned obliquely to the wall and his hindquarters to the inside (fig. 115). The horse remains slightly bent around the rider's

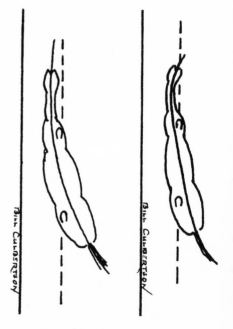

Fig. 115. Haunches-in is a more difficult movement for the horse to perform than shoulder-in. Left: Correct position. Right: Incorrect position.

inside leg. The horse looks in the direction of travel, and his outside legs pass and cross in front of the inside legs. The angle to the wall should be 30 to 33 degrees. This exercise is more difficult to perform than the shoulder-in; it takes a strong rider to keep the horse properly bent with the haunches remaining to the inside.

AIDS TO HAUNCHES-IN

Both reins must be used to keep the horse's forehand on the track. The outside rein exerts the most influence, its action being supported by the inside rein and the rider's outside leg. The rider's weight remains to the inside, and the inside leg remains on the girth to push the horse foreward and maintain the bend. The outside leg is positioned behind the girth to push the horse's hindquarters away from the wall, causing the horse's outside hind leg to step over and in front of the inside hind leg.

ARENA EXERCISES

Perform haunches-in in both directions along the long side of the arena. Practice first at the walk and then at the trot.

Common Problems

1. *The horse is not uniformly bent from poll to tail.* Check the rein length (too short or too long) and increase or decrease the bend in the horse's body so that the bend in the head and neck, defined through the position of the reins, and the bend in the horse's body achieved through active leg aids are the same.

2. *The horse is not looking in the direction of travel.* Check the rider's upper-body position for twisting, the position of the hands, and the rein length. The inside rein may need to be shortened,

and the outside rein lengthened proportionately.

3. *The horse loses impulsion causing an irregular gait.* Have the rider lessen the degree of bend in the horse's body. The more acute the bend, the more difficult it is for the horse to maintain impulsion. Sufficient impulsion will result in a regular footfall pattern, providing the rider is pushing the horse forward into a quiet and steady bend. If the rider's hands cannot function independently of his seat, jerking hand movements can also alter the horse's footfall pattern and result in an irregular gait. Once the degree of bend has been reduced, impulsion has been reestablished, and the hands have resumed a quiet and steady position, have the rider concentrate on the use of active leg aids and riding the haunches-in with only a slight degree of bend.

4. *There is insufficient crossing over to define two distinct tracks.* Check the rider's basic leg position. If the legs have fallen too far to the rear, the faulty position can result in lack of sideways motion. Increase use of the outside leg, pressing and releasing to push the horse sideways. The inside leg remains at the girth to maintain the bend and sufficient impulsion.

5. *The horse displays incorrect flexion and head carriage.* An inexperienced rider may exert a sideways and upward pressure on the inside rein, causing the horse to twist his head to the side. The position of the ears becomes unlevel, the nose turns to the side, and the horse's head is no longer at a vertical angle to the ground. To correct this problem, point out to the rider the incorrect position of the horse's head. Then have the rider readjust the hand position to eliminate the sideways and upward pull on the inside rein. The rider may need to lower the inside hand and maintain the correct head and neck position by gently squeezing the inside rein, the inside hand

remaining close to the horse's neck and not exerting an upward pull.

Haunches-Out (Renvers)

Haunches-out is the reverse position of haunches-in; that is, the horse travels with his tail to the wall rather than his head to the wall (fig. 116). The horse looks in the direction of travel and performs this movement with the same degree of bend as in the haunches-in position. Technically there is no difference between the movements. Only the horse's position differs in its relationship to the wall along which it is traveling. The aids, degree of bend, comments, and common problems in haunches-in are also applicable to haunches-out.

Care must be taken not to overbend horses during the early stages of training. It is essential for the rider to maintain sufficient impulsion and to begin with only a slight bend in the horse's body so

as to maintain forward and sideways movement. While a finished horse performs haunches-in and haunches-out at a 30- to 33-degree angle to the wall, asking the horse to travel with that degree of bend will result in the loss of impulsion at first. Remember that, when teaching and practicing any lateral movement, the more acute the bend in a horse's body, the more difficult it is for the horse to achieve and maintain sufficient impulsion. Maintaining impulsion is the first consideration, while the degree of bend is increased slowly until the desired angle with the wall is reached. Sufficient impulsion, regular gait, and correct bend will be achieved through many patient practice sessions.

Common Problems

The problems related to performing haunches-out are the same as those associated with haunches-in. Review the common problems discussed in "Haunches-In" above.

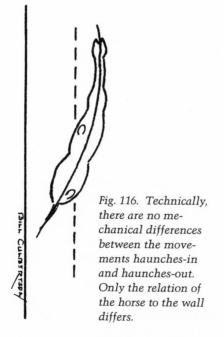

Fig. 116. Technically, there are no mechanical differences between the movements haunches-in and haunches-out. Only the relation of the horse to the wall differs.

Chapter 10

Counter Canter

Counter canter, or false lead, is a suppling exercise that requires a horse to canter a circle in one direction while maintaining the opposite, or counter, lead. For example, a horse performing a counter canter canters a circle to the right while maintaining the left lead. This exercise helps develop smoothness and balance in the horse and requires the rider to coordinate the use of the aids. Counter canter is also essential to prepare the horse for the flying change of lead.

The counter-canter exercise may be introduced when the horse is well balanced and relaxed during all exercises performed at the true canter and students are able to coordinate the aids required for the proper execution of leg yielding and turn on the forehand.

AIDS TO COUNTER CANTER

Counter canter is ridden just as a true canter is ridden. The rider uses the same seat and the same aids. The bend in the horse is in the direction of the lead. The only difference between the counter canter and the true canter is that the horse may be bent left, for example, traveling on the left lead, but performing a circle to the right (fig. 117). To execute a counter canter to the right, the rider uses the aids for a circle to the left— horse bent to the left, traveling on the left lead, the rider's weight remaining to the inside of the circle. From this position the rider pushes out with the inside leg, maintaining the horse on the outside rein, which leads the horse to the right. Throughout this exercise the horse should remain balanced and work at a three-beat rhythmic gait. The rider must sit in a vertical position and not allow the seat to be pulled forward from the saddle. Sufficient impulsion and coordination of aids must be maintained to help balance the horse and free the forehand and leading legs of weight.

125

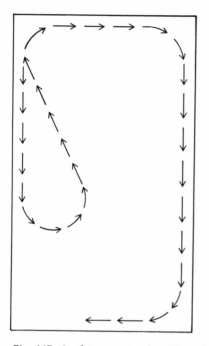

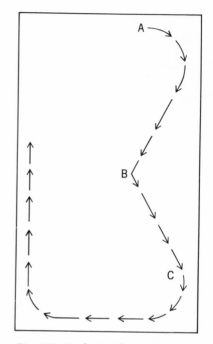

Fig. 117. In this exercise the rider asks for a canter on the left lead and maintains the lead through the half-turn and along the long wall. Corners are kept round and shallow. If a rider has trouble maintaining the counter canter, he may ride the counter canter along the long side of the arena and end the exercise by dropping to a trot before reaching the corner.

Fig. 118. To begin this exercise, the rider trots on the right rein between A and B. At B the rider applies the aids for the canter. At C the rider pushes the horse around the arena on the false lead.

ARENA EXERCISES

1. The easiest way to introduce the counter canter is to ask a student to begin cantering down a long side of the arena on the correct lead, half-halt, and then ride a half-turn. As the horse returns to the long side, the rider maintains the aids and canters around the arena on the counter lead. The rider must maintain shallow corners and leave adequate room between the horse and the arena wall. This exercise is practiced on both reins.

2. A student is asked to ride at a trot through a corner and diagonally toward the center of the arena. Upon reaching the center of the arena, the rider turns the horse toward the long side, applies the aids for the counter lead, canters toward the rail, and maintains the counter canter around the arena (fig. 118).

At first, horses may tend to break gait during these exercises owing to lack of balance or rider error. When this occurs, have the rider quietly repeat the exercise without punishing the horse. If the horse is punished for breaking gait, he will likely assume the lead for the true canter to regain his balance, an undesirable reaction when the counter canter is being taught. The student should correct the horse's mistake but should not punish him for the error. The instructor must see that all the figures ridden in the counter canter remain large to help horse and rider maintain their balance.

Common Problems

1. *The horse loses balance and travels too fast.* The rider must maintain aid emphasis and sitting-bone influence throughout the exercise. The half-halt is employed to regulate the horse's gait. The correct position of the rider is essential to prevent the horse from losing his balance and falling on his forehand.

2. *The horse begins to travel on the forehand and lean on the bit.* Too fast a pace, lack of balance, or too small a figure can cause a horse to fall on his forehand. The rider should be sure that his position and aid emphasis are correct.

3. *The horse shows a tendency to change leads.* Check the rider's application of aids and sitting-bone influence. If the horse changes leads, the rider should execute a quiet transition to trot and then repeat the exercise. This problem will be eliminated when the horse increases his balance and degree of suppleness and when the rider becomes steady, uses the correct aids, and maintains correct inside-sitting-bone influence.

4. *The horse is overbent to the inside.* The rider should lengthen the inside rein and shorten the outside rein to straighten the horse so that no more than the outside corner of the inside eye is visible. The rider should maintain contact on the outside rein to limit the bend and help support the horse's movement.

5. *The horse is bent in the wrong direction.* Have the rider shorten the inside rein and lengthen the outside rein to allow the horse to assume the correct bend. A complete review of all aid application is recommended so that the rider understands the correct physical outline of the horse and the aids required to help maintain the proper shape.

6. *The rider is incorrectly positioned in the saddle.* The rider's weight must stay to the inside of the bend, the rider's inside leg pushing the horse to the outside rein.

7. *The rider makes insufficient use of aids.* Encourage the student to work to coordinate leg, hand, and sitting-bone influences during the exercise. All aids must be maintained throughout the exercise to enable the horse to perform correctly.

Chapter 11

The Flying Change of Lead

The flying change of lead is the change of leg, or lead, performed by the horse at the canter without breaking gait. It is considered an advanced movement. The difficulty of the flying change lies in the timing for correct aid application to allow the horse to make the change.

The horse performs the flying change of lead during the moment of suspension, the fourth, silent beat of the canter. A horse performing a flying change from the left lead to the right lead does so using the footfall sequence shown in figures 119 and 120.

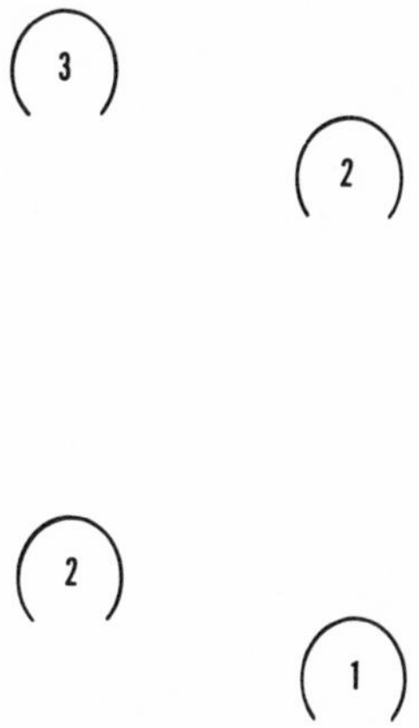

Fig. 119. Left lead to moment of suspension—all four feet off ground—flying change occurs here—to . . . (see Fig. 120).

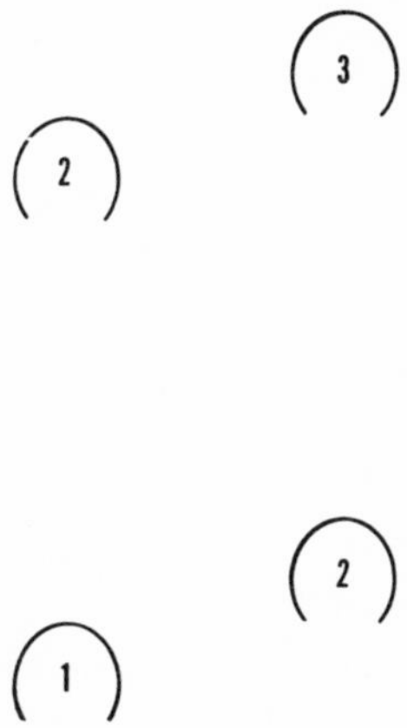

Fig. 120. . . . right lead.

Timing

The footfall sequence and lead are determined by the position of the horse's hind legs, for one hind leg serves as the first beat of the canter. Correct aid application must occur before the moment of suspension to allow the horse to respond and initiate the new lead, which demands a change in the position of the hind legs.

Because the rider must apply the aids and allow time for the horse to respond, the timing—when to ask for the flying change—is of major importance. Correct application of the aids depends somewhat on the rider and horse performing the movement, for both horse and rider respond to the situation with different reaction times. The most advantageous time for aid application is usually when the leading front leg is on the ground. This is the third beat of the canter, which is followed by the moment of suspension when the change occurs. If horse and rider cannot respond that quickly, the aids can be applied sooner, during the second beat of the canter, when the diagonal pair of legs is on the ground. A certain amount of experimentation may be required; the key, however, is to be sure that the students are applying the aids to allow for sufficient response *before* the moment of suspension occurs.

Preparation

Success in achieving the flying change depends on the methodical training and preparation the horse has received. The horse must be supple and balanced. He must be immediately responsive to canter aids and be able to increase or decrease the tempo of the gait. He should exhibit sufficient impulsion with a degree of collection during work at the canter and should execute a balanced, smooth counter canter in both directions. The horse should also be able to perform

a simple change of lead, dropping to trot and walk before assuming the new lead. If horse and rider have mastered these exercises, they should be sufficiently prepared to execute a flying change.

AIDS

The aids for the flying change are the same as those for a correct canter departure. Since the aids will be applied at a precise moment, the rider's outside leg is moved behind the girth before the aids are actively applied so that the change signal will not be late. For example, a rider on the left rein at the canter would have the inside (left) leg at the girth and the outside (right) leg behind the girth. Before the aids for the flying change are applied, the rider slides the left leg behind the girth so that it is ready when the precise moment of aid application occurs. If the rider waits to move the leg until the designated moment of aid application, the leg aid will be too late.

The rider's outside leg signals the flying change. The rider's inside leg remains at the girth unless the horse throws his haunches to the inside. If that occurs, the rider moves the inside leg behind the girth to help prevent the action. The rider's upper body remains erect, and the rider looks straight ahead, not down, to remain in balance with the horse. The rider must be careful not to retard the horse's action through unnecessary and prolonged rein pressure. As the leg aids are changed, the rider squeezes the new outside rein to tell the horse to plant the outside hind foot. Immediately after this signal, the rein must be relaxed so that the horse has freedom to execute the flying change.

When the student begins the flying-change exercises, have a person on the ground to watch the position of the horse's hind feet as they are set down. Some horses will bring both hind legs under them at the same time instead of initiating the new lead with the outside hindfoot. Horses that bring both hind legs under them at the same time change their lead first in front and then behind, a fault that causes a choppy, jerky change lacking the desired rhythmic quality. To correct this problem, have the rider increase the pressure from the outside leg, behind the girth. A whip may also be used to reinforce the leg action if the horse does not respond.

ARENA EXERCISES

Flying changes are more easily performed on a circular track, because a circle provides the horse with the correct bend when the flying change is made from counter canter to true canter. To help keep the horse calm, the rider should allow him to walk quietly on a long rein after performing each change. Keep practice sessions short, no more than fifteen to twenty minutes.

1. The easiest way to teach a flying change is to make a change from counter canter to a true canter on a large circle. Have the students ride a full circle in counter canter to establish the rhythm. At a designated point have them apply the aids for the flying change and make the change to the true canter (fig. 121). Make the changes from counter canter to

true canter at varying points on the circle to prevent the horse from anticipating the lead change.

2. A flying change may be made from one circle to another (fig. 122).

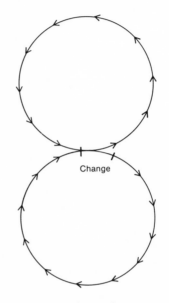

Fig. 122. *Flying change from one circle to another.*

3. The horse may be asked to canter a half-turn and, upon reaching the track, execute a flying change (fig. 123).

4. Serpentines provide another exercise to practice the flying change. As the horse changes direction, he executes the flying change (fig. 124).

5. When a horse can perform a flying change on a circular track consistently, with freedom of movement and without loss of tempo, then flying changes can be executed on straight lines. To execute a flying change across the diagonal, have the student ride the horse through a corner and across the diagonal and execute the flying change upon reaching the track (fig. 125).

6. To execute a flying change on the centerline, the student rides the horse

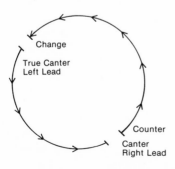

Fig. 121. *Counter canter to true canter.*

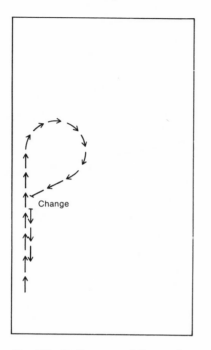

Fig. 123. Half-turn and flying change.

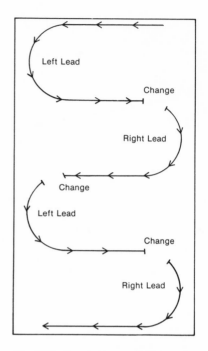

Fig. 124. Serpentine and flying change.

up the centerline and executes a flying change upon reaching the opposite short side of the arena (fig. 126).

Common Problems

1. *The horse lacks impulsion.* Have the rider increase the use of the leg aids and send the horse forward, being sure that the rider is not balancing or pulling on the reins to impede the forward motion of the horse. Reemphasize that no movement can be performed correctly without *first* establishing a sufficient degree of impulsion and forward movement.

2. *The horse's hind feet are together on a change; the lead change occurs first in front.* The horse must respond to applied pressure by moving away from the pressure before the flying change is introduced. The turn on the forehand and lateral movements are used to accomplish this purpose. Sideways

pressure applied by the rider's outside leg positioned behind the girth is the aid that initiates a change in the position of the horse's hind feet during the flying change. If the horse does not consistently respond to applied pressure by moving away from it, or if insufficient pressure (leg aid) is applied, the horse may bring both hind legs under him at the same time and initiate a front lead change first. Remind the students that a horse that initiates a flying change with the correct hind leg will follow through with the correct footfall pattern and correct leading front leg. The reverse of this situation is not true. Horses that execute a flying change by picking up the lead front foot first will not necessarily follow through and change correctly behind. This incorrect footfall pattern is described as "cross cantering" or "disunited."

Insufficient or incorrect contact or use

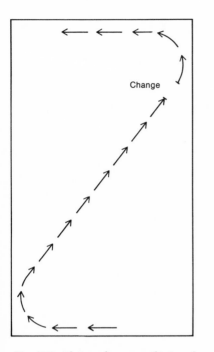

Fig. 125. Flying change utilizing the diagonal.

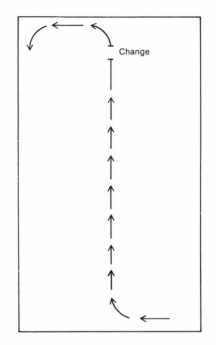

Fig. 126. Flying change utilizing the centerline.

of the reins may also cause a horse to plant both hind feet simultaneously and change in front and not behind. An incorrect bend in the horse or lack of a support rein to help the horse execute a correct hind change first can also cause this problem.

3. *The horse is not properly prepared for the flying change.* Suppling exercises or a single track and lateral movements are necessary preparatory exercises for the flying change. A horse must willingly move away from pressure and be supple and balanced when traveling on either rein before the flying-change exercise is feasible.

4. *The rider twists the upper body.* This problem often occurs when a weak rider tries to increase the pressure applied by the inside leg when attempting to bend the horse. Ask the rider to "raise your inside shoulder" or "lower your

outside shoulder." When the shoulders are held in a level position, the hip will not collapse. Holding a small amount of air in the lungs also helps elevate the rib cage and prevent a collapsed hip. Remind riders to "sit tall" and not look down when executing a flying change, since the correct position of the rider will help the horse maintain his balance.

5. *The rider attempts a flying change by throwing the weight from side to side.* The rider must learn to use the correct leg and rein aids to execute the flying change. If a rider attempts a flying change by throwing the weight from side to side, the horse must compensate for this unsteady burden by moving under the rider's weight and reaching out with a front leg to maintain his balance. This action (rider) and reaction (horse) can cause a horse to change his lead in front but not behind. In other

words, lack of leg aids from the rider equals no hind-leg change from the horse.

6. *The rider looks down to watch the position of the front legs during the change.* If the rider looks down rather than straight ahead over the horse's ears, total balance is greatly altered, and the rider's ability to use the aids is decreased. Anatomically, when a rider looks down, the weight and forward position of the head cause the spine to become round. The pelvis rotates forward, pulling the sitting bones up and out of the saddle, minimizing the weight influence of the rider's seat. The correct position of the upper body is drastically altered, the end result being incorrectly placed weight and insufficient use of the aids, which adversely affect the horse's balance and ability to perform.

7. *The rider makes insufficient use of the outside leg.* The rider's outside leg must be used to initiate the flying change. Failure to use sufficient outside leg pressure to initiate a hind-leg change can result in the horse changing in front but not behind.

8. *Pressure on the reins restricts the horse's freedom of movement.* The rider must maintain contact on the reins and position the horse correctly in the direction of travel, but undue pressure or backward pull on the reins must be avoided because it will restrict the horse's forward movement.

Conclusion

"Look first to yourself for the mistake and then to the horse" is the principle underlying this book. Thorough knowledge of the basic principles and methodically learned skills are the tools that allow the rider to discover, examine, and analyze mistakes. Recognizing and accepting that rider error constitutes 95 percent of all riding problems allow one to begin to learn the science of riding.

Just as without knowledge one cannot learn or understand, so without development of a feel for the horse's rhythmic stride one cannot successfully ride or teach the art. Knowledge and understanding, plus long hours of dedicated work, combine to make the true horseman and horsewoman, and to this end we must dedicate ourselves if we are truly to master the equestrian art.

Appendices

Appendix A

Parts of the Saddle and Bridle

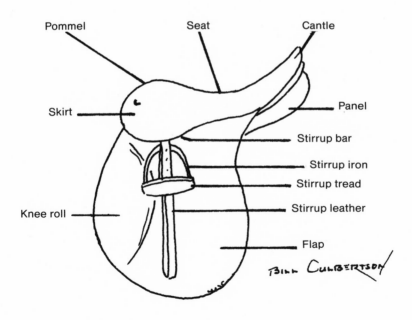

Fig. A.1. Parts of the saddle.

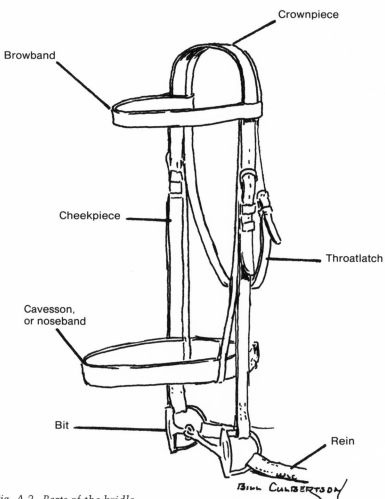

Crownpiece

Browband

Cheekpiece

Throatlatch

Cavesson,
or noseband

Bit

Rein

BILL CULBERTSON

Fig. A.2. Parts of the bridle.

Appendix B

Basic School Movements

1. Cross the school

2. Up the centerline

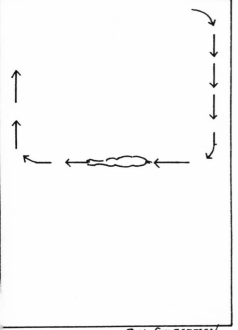
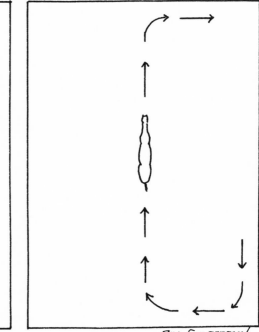

Fig. B.1. Movement in which horse and rider turn widthwise across the school, riding from one long side of the arena to the other.

Fig. B.2. Movement in which horse and rider travel up the centerline the full length of the school, riding from one short side of the arena to the other.

3. Cross the diagonal

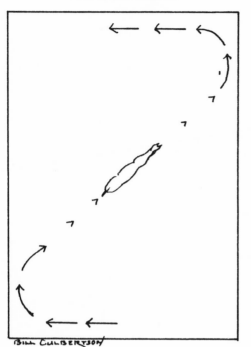

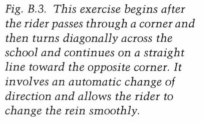

Fig. B.3. This exercise begins after the rider passes through a corner and then turns diagonally across the school and continues on a straight line toward the opposite corner. It involves an automatic change of direction and allows the rider to change the rein smoothly.

4. Full turn

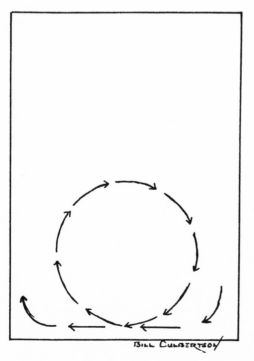

Fig. B.4. Full turn, or circle, is accomplished when horse and rider complete a 360-degree turn. Full turns should remain large until the later stages of training.

5. Half-turn

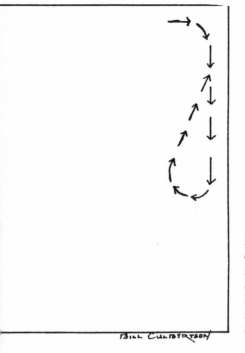

BILL CULBERTSON

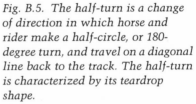

Fig. B.5. The half-turn is a change of direction in which horse and rider make a half-circle, or 180-degree turn, and travel on a diagonal line back to the track. The half-turn is characterized by its teardrop shape.

6. Serpentine

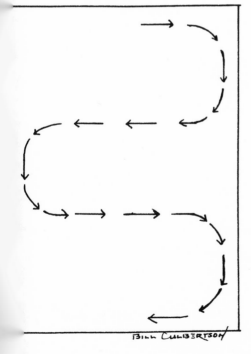

BILL CULBERTSON

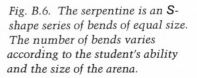

Fig. B.6. The serpentine is an S-shape series of bends of equal size. The number of bends varies according to the student's ability and the size of the arena.

7. Change of rein

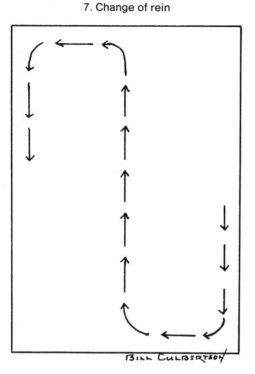

BILL CULBERTSON

Fig. B.7. An example of the change of rein or change of direction is the half-turn and cross-the-diagonal.

8. Change of rein across the school

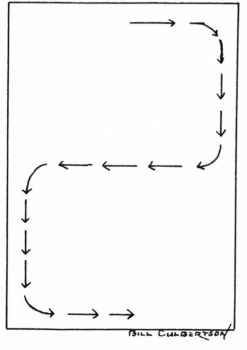

BILL CULBERTSON

Fig. B.8. Up-the-centerline and cross-the-school may also be performed with a change of rein.

Appendix C

Footfall Sequences

$\left(2\right)$ $\left(4\right)$

$\left(1\right)$ $\left(3\right)$

Fig. C.1. Walk.

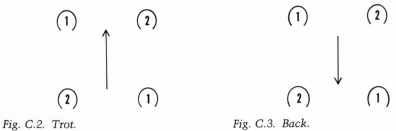

Fig. C.2. Trot.   *Fig. C.3. Back.*

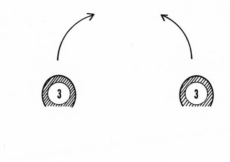

Fig. C.4. Canter.

Appendix D

Sample Safety and Conduct Rules

Note: These rules were formulated for rider protection and for the protection of all persons using the horses at an equine facility.

General Rules

1. In all appropriate classes straps on hard hats are to be down and fastened.
2. If any kind of problem occurs, call an instructor.
3. Return all tack and grooming aids to designated areas.
4. Observe the dress code [see Appendix F] at all times.
5. Keep all gates and snap locks on pens fastened at all times.
6. Smoking is not permitted.
7. Ask any unescorted stranger if you can help him or direct him to the office.
8. There is to be no running or joking in the arena.

Horse-handling Safety

1. Before approaching a horse, be sure that he is aware of your presence. Approach him from the left side at a three-quarter angle to his shoulder and then halter him.
2. Do not approach a horse if your are wearing a flapping coat or jacket. Be sure that outer garments are securely fastened to prevent startling the horse.
3. If you find a horse in any trouble, *call a staff member.* Do not try to help the horse yourself.
4. Never stand directly in front of a horse except when you are braiding the forelock.
5. Mane and tail pulling and clipping are to be done only under the supervision of an instructor.
6. Horses are not to be ridden in the barn or pens.

7. If you hose off a horse at the wash-rack, never stand in front of him or spray him in the face.
8. Never sit down when holding a horse.
9. Lead all horses with a lead rope or stud shank with the snap fastened to the ring in the halter.
10. When leading a horse, position yourself beside his shoulder.
11. When leading a horse, hold the shank or reins correctly, using both hands.
12. When leading a horse, do not stop to chat with another student or allow the horse to graze.
13. No student is to mount up for riding until an instructor is at the arena.
14. Shout, "Avoid the gate!" when you enter an arena already occupied by moving horses.
15. Bareback riding is not permitted.
16. Students are never to remove jackets, scarves, or other clothing while mounted. Dismount to take off excess clothing.
17. If a bridle must be changed with another horse in the arena area, *both* horses are to have halters and lead ropes around their necks for control purposes while the change is being made.
18. When horses are lined up for any reason, they are to be no closer than fifteen feet apart.

Hitch-Rail Safety

1. All horses are to be tied with a safety quick-release knot.
2. No more than two horses are to be tied on one side of a hitch rail at the same time. Stagger the spacing of horses on both sides of the hitch rail so that they are not tied directly across from each other. Do not tie a horse so close to the end of the hitch rail that he can walk around the end and snug himself up on the other side.
3. Never go between a horse and the hitch rail. Speak to the horse, stay close to him, and walk around back.
4. Never place tack on the hitch rail.
5. Do not slap a horse on his hind-quarters. Do not lean against a horse.
6. Do not kneel beside a horse when working on his legs or feet.
7. All horses are to be comfort-groomed and hoof-flexed (when necessary) before being penned.
8. *Never return a hot horse to his pen.* Hand-walk the horse to cool him and intermittently offer him a few sips of water until he is cool and no longer overly thirsty.
9. Do not ground-tie any horse.
10. Never tie a horse with the reins. Always use a halter and a lead rope.
11. Never leave grooming aids on the ground at the hitch rail. Return brushes, curry combs, and other equipment to their designated areas.

Appendix E

Sample Safety Quiz

1. After checking the girth, a rider may mount up and begin warm-up exercises with or without an instructor present. T or F (Circle one.)
2. Horses are never to be positioned closer than ____ feet apart to avoid problem situations.
3. Shout, "____ ____ ____!" when you enter the arena and riders are already warming up on the rail.
4. A rider must never ride in clothing that is loose and flapping. T or F
5. A rider must dismount when taking off a jacket. T or F
6. Generally speaking, a horse should never be tied with the reins. T or F
7. It is permissible to place tack on the hitch rail when returning to the tack room for another item. T or F
8. Horses are tied with a knot called a

____ ____.
9. All pen gates are to be ____ at all times.
10. Never go between the front of the horse and the hitch rail. T or F
11. Kneeling beside a horse is permitted when working on the feet and legs. T or F
12. All horses are to be ____ ____ and ____ before being put away.
13. A horse should be approached at a ____ angle to his shoulder.
14. When leading a horse, the rider should hold the lead shank or reins correctly, using both hands. T or F
15. Horses should be ____ at the hitch rail so they are not directly across from each other.
16. In most instances only ____ horse(s) should be tied on each side of the hitch rails.

Appendix F

Sample Dress Code

In compliance with [school or organization] safety regulations, a minimum dress code has been established in an effort to afford physical protection and convey a professional image of all individuals (faculty, staff, and students) involved in any activity in the teaching facility. Any time an individual is pursuing an activity on the premises, he or she is expected to abide by the minimum dress standards set forth below:

1. *Adequate dress* includes either jeans or western long pants suitable for riding or working around horses. English breeches and boots may be worn. Shorts are not permitted.

Long- and short-sleeve shirts, sport shirts, and T-shirts are acceptable attire. Halter tops and tank tops are not considered acceptable attire for those working with horses in an academic environment.

2. *Adequate footwear* includes western or English boots or shoes with hard soles and sufficient heels to enable the rider to obtain proper foot placement in a stirrup and to work safely around horses when dismounted. Tennis shoes, moccasins, sandals, thongs, and similar soft footwear are not permitted.

3. It is hoped that each person involved in the equitation program will take pride in his or her appearance. The teaching facility is readily available for public inspection, and many visitors tour the facility. Faculty, staff, and students should realize that a neat personal appearance is of utmost importance.

Appendix G

Bounce-Pad Construction

Bounce pads are made from round or square pieces of foam rubber commonly used in small throw pillows. They are available already cut in one-half-, three-quarter-, and 1-inch thicknesses at local fabric, hobby-supply, discount, or surplus stores. Round ones are a little easier to use. Invest in one or two sizes and then take them home. Saddle the horse and decide which size will make the saddle sit just a little higher than level. Remember, as the rider sinks into the saddle, the foam-rubber pad loses some of its airiness.

To position the pad, lift up the back of the saddle and place the bounce pad *on top* of the regular pad so that its foremost part is under the middle portion of the saddle seat. It will then extend backward elevating the back of the saddle to the proper height. Once satisfied that the pad is the correct thickness, outline the back of the saddle on the bounce pad, using a felt-tip pen. Remove the pad and cut off the edges that protrude from under the saddle.

If the saddle is new or if the horse tends to have a low back, it may be necessary

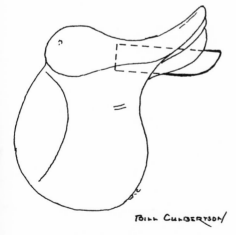

Fig. G.1. When properly placed, the bounce pad helps rest the saddle in a level position on the horse's back.

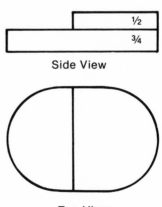

Side View

Top View

Fig. G.2. Side and top views of the bounce pad.

to make a special bounce pad. To make this special pad the exact height needed, begin with a three-quarter-inch bounce pad and place a one-half-inch pad on top of it. Cut the one-half-inch pad in half. Place one half of the thinner pad on top of and at the back of the thicker pad. Glue in place. This pad will elevate the rear of the saddle as much as needed without unduly increasing the thickness of the pad that extends under the rider's seat. Remember, the object is to elevate the *back* of the saddle.

Bounce pads are a great aid for English riders. In addition to adjusting a saddle into a level position, it provides a horse's back with extra cushion when the rider executes a sitting trot or an extended gait. It helps absorb unintentional shock when a novice gets left behind going over a jump or sits down in the saddle too soon upon landing. Most of all, a bounce pad is a courtesy to school horses ridden by novices who are learning to ride and with whom the "beginner bounce" is inevitable.

Appendix H

AHSA Training Level, Tests 1 and 2

AHSA Training Level, Test 1 (1979)

1.	*A*	Enter working trot (sitting).
	X	Halt through the walk; salute. Proceed working trot (sitting) through the walk.
	C	Track to the right.
2.	*M*	Working trot (rising).
	A	Working trot (sitting), circle right 20-m. diameter.
3.	*A*	Working canter, right lead. Circle 20-m. diameter once around.
4.	*A*	Straight ahead.
	E	Working trot (sitting).
5.	*M* X *K*	Change rein working trot (rising).
6.	*A*	Working trot (sitting), circle left 20-m. diameter.
7.	*A*	Working canter, left lead. Circle 20-m. diameter once around.
8.	*B*	Working trot (sitting).
	C	Working walk.
9.	*H* X *F*	Working walk.
	F	Working trot (sitting).
10.	*A*	Down centerline.
	X	Halt through the walk; salute. Leave arena free walk on loose rein.

AHSA Training Level, Test 2 (1979)

1. *A*	Enter working trot (sitting).	
X	Halt through the walk; salute. Proceed working trot (sitting) through the walk.	
C	Track to the left.	
2. *E*	Circle left 20-m. diameter.	
3. *A*	Down centerline.	
C	Track to the right.	
4. *B*	Circle right 20-m. diameter.	
5. between *F* and *A*	Working canter, right lead.	
6. *E*	Circle right 20-m. diameter, once around then straight ahead.	
M	Working trot (sitting).	
7. *B*	Turn to the right.	
E	Track to the left.	
8. between *K* and *A*	Working canter, left lead.	
9. *B*	Circle left 20-m. diameter, once around then straight ahead.	
M	Working trot (sitting).	
10. *C*	Working walk.	
H X F	Change rein, free walk on a loose rein.	
F	Working walk.	
11. *A*	Down centerline.	
D	Working trot (sitting).	
G	Halt through the walk; salute. Leave arena, free walk on a loose rein.	

Appendix I

Cavalletti Spacing (General)

Gait	Space Between Cavalletti
Strong walk:	2'8''–3'6''
Extended walk:	3'9''
Ordinary trot:	4'3''–4'10''
Extended trot:	increase a few inches
Collected trot:	3'8''–4'3''
Ordinary canter:	9'–12'

Appendix J

Cavalletti Construction

The use of cavalletti originated with an Italian cavalry officer, Captain Frederico Caprilli. The father of forward-seat riding, Caprilli worked horses at the trot and canter over wooden rails of varying height to increase the horses' balance and muscular development. These wooden rails, secured on firm low stands, were the first cavalletti.

Rails used in the construction of cavalletti must be thick, round, and hard so that they will not splinter when hit. Rails should be a uniform length, preferably six to nine feet. The longer the rail, the more difficult it is to keep the horse traveling on a straight line when working through a cavalletti series. Each rail should be secured in two low endpieces made in the shape of an X so that the cavalletti can be rotated to three different heights. Properly constructed,

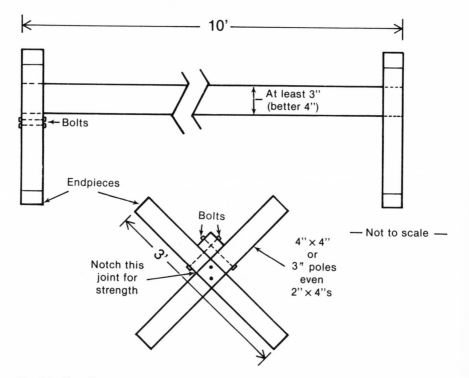

Fig. J.1. Cavalletti construction plans.

the endpieces position the cavalletti at the height of a ground pole, a trot pole (six to eight inches high), and a cantering pole (approximately 18 inches high). Creative use of six to nine cavalletti can provide sufficient gymnastic exercises for horse and rider at the walk, trot, and canter.

Cavalletti are usually painted white. A wide strip of color, red, blue, or green, can be painted in a band on either side of the center to aid the horse in traveling a straight line through the complete cavalletti series.

Suggested Reading

Klimke, Reiner. *Cavalletti*. London: A. A. Allen and Co., 1976.

Ljungquist, Bengt. *Practical Dressage Manual*. Richmond, Va.: Press of Whittet and Shepperson, 1976.

Morris, George H. *Hunter Seat Equitation*. Garden City, N.Y.: Doubleday and Co., 1971.

Museler, Wilhelm. *Riding Logic*. London: Eyre Methuen, 1973.

Podhajsky, Alois. *The Complete Training of Horse and Rider*. Garden City, N.Y.: Doubleday and Co., 1967.

Smythe, R. H. *The Mind of the Horse*. Barttleboro, Vt.: Stephen Greene Press, 1965.

Stanier, Sylvia. *The Art of Lungeing*. London: J. A. Allen and Co., 1976.

Wilcox, Sheila. *The Event Horse*. Philadelphia, Pa.: A. B. Lippincott Co.

Index

159